LB
2369
.B49
2007

A Practical Guide to the Qualitative Dissertation

*Sari Knopp Biklen and
Ronnie Casella*

TEACHERS
COLLEGE
PRESS

Teachers College, Columbia University
New York and London

Published by Teachers College Press, 1234 Amsterdam Avenue, New York, NY 10027

Copyright © 2007 by Teachers College, Columbia University

All rights reserved. No part of this publication may be reproduced or transmitted in any form or by any means, electronic or mechanical, including photocopy, or any information storage and retrieval system, without permission from the publisher.

Library of Congress Cataloging-in-Publication Data
Biklen, Sari Knopp.
     A practical guide to the qualitative dissertation / Sari Knopp Biklen and Ronnie Casella.
          p.   cm.
     Includes bibliographical references and index.
     ISBN 978-0-8077-4760-5 (pbk : alk. paper)
     1. Dissertations, Academic—Handbooks, manuals, etc.   2. Report writing—Handbooks, manuals, etc.   I. Casella, Ronnie, 1963–   II. Title.

     LB2369.B49 2007
     808.02—dc22

                                                                                          2006101180

ISBN 978-0-8077-4760-5 (paper)

Printed on acid-free paper
Manufactured in the United States of America

14   13   12   11   10   09   08   07   8   7   6   5   4   3   2   1

For all of the
qualitative researchers we have learned from—both
the old hats and the new apprentices—and in
honor of the social change their work engenders

Contents

Acknowledgments

Many people contributed to this book, and some of them do not know it. We thank them anyway even though there are too many of them to name individually. We could only write a book like this because of the many wonderful experiences we have had over the years working with doctoral students on their dissertations. So while this work was part of our jobs as professors, we also became students of the process of dissertation writing.

Students who took the Advanced Seminar in Qualitative Research over the years raised many questions about dissertation writing, and brought their own struggles out for discussion and for advice. These seminars were particularly important for this book. They taught us what kinds of questions doctoral students care about when they write their dissertations, and what kinds of questions we want them to care about. The seminar members from fall 2004 and 2005 were kind enough to offer feedback on drafts of individual chapters, and to contribute edits for some of the chapters (for classes on writing and editing).

We interviewed a number of students and former students and used the writings from students' proposals and former students' dissertations to illustrate a number of the points we make in this text. Thank you to Allison Alden, Cerri Banks, Jennifer Bannister, Amy Best, Lesley Bogad, Dennis Culhane, Joe DeVitis, Jennifer Esposito, Kayde Flower-Kim, Kathleen Farrell, Douglas Green, Katherine Gregory, Britt Hamre, Chris Kliewer, Kristen Luschen, Kristy McGowan, Jeff Mangram, Jodi Mullen, Joanne O'Toole, Jeanette Rhedding-Jones, Robin Riley, Terri Ruyter, Todd Sodano, Michael Schwartz, Brenda Solomon, Larry Stedman, Linda Steet, Raji Swaminathan, Amy Tweedy, Linda Waldron, Dara Wexler, Tian Yu, and Julie Zuckerman.

The faculty we interviewed were particularly helpful. Steve Taylor was forthright and informative about Institutional Review Boards and professional ethics. He is also an outstanding chair of the IRB at Syracuse

University, partly because he is an experienced qualitative researcher himself and knows the IRB regulations extremely well. He is interested in ethics rather than bureaucracy. Marj DeVault, Beth Ferri, and Celia Oyler offered their views on dissertation writing, and were thoughtful and insightful about the processes connected with the nontraditional dissertation particularly. Thanks so much for your insights and discussions of your experiences.

Barb Maphey was helpful in a speedy way about dissertation forms and processes. Maryann Barker and Dani Weinstein provided scanning and copying services in addition to all the invisible labor office staff perform. Thank you. Carol Saltz is such a superb editor and director of Teachers College Press. Thanks for your flexibility, your demands, and your support, particularly this time. Judy Berman was terrific to work with over the last year.

And Doug Biklen listened to many accounts of class and discussions about dissertations and was his usual supportive self.

A Practical Guide to the Qualitative Dissertation

CHAPTER 1

Thinking About the Dissertation

Writing a good qualitative dissertation really demands only three things of you: a good idea, rich data that you analyze thoughtfully, and the discipline to write a finished product. Of course, there are other "little" things that do make a difference: an examining committee that understands what qualitative research is; a good relationship with your dissertation advisor; a topic that is not out of favor at the time you are writing about it; and a personal life where major health, family, or financial problems don't get in the way. And there is one more issue: the politics of your topic. Academics often disagree with each other about what is significant, what ideas are acceptable, and how topics ought to be approached. Students doing controversial work on politically volatile topics around race, gender, class, sexuality, and ability sometimes face difficulties. But if you can surmount the first three challenges, you can figure out strategies to handle most other things.

We have either worked with doctoral students for many years or been one pretty recently, so between us we have heard many stories about all of the issues raised in the last paragraph. We will talk about some of these tales, but this is not a book of war stories or complaints or a narrative of how tough it is to finish a dissertation. Rather, this is a book about how to think about some of the different concerns that arise during the course of doing a dissertation. It is not a book about how to do qualitative research. There are a number of good texts already available for you to turn to for advice about the process of doing the research and that describe what qualitative research is (e.g., Bogdan & Biklen, 2007; Denzin & Lincoln, 1994; Rubin & Rubin, 1995), and we have listed some of these in the Resource Guide at the end of this book. As we have said, this is a book about both how to think about the primary tasks involved in writing a qualitative dissertation and how you might consider problems that often arise.

Campuses are peopled with dissertation experts. Your dissertation chair, dissertation committee members, other faculty, post-docs, professional staff—these are some of them. They are often sources of good advice. Part of your work as a doctoral student intent on writing a good dissertation is to figure out what kinds of advice you can get from these different people. Some are good at giving you resources to look at. Others can read your work well and give you the kind of criticism you need. Still others can offer you a pep talk that helps you, when your motivation or energy wavers, to generate enthusiasm for your work once again.

Communicating with others about your dissertation is important. We had a brilliant student in our department who was probably writing a brilliant dissertation. But he wrote in isolation, never communicating with anyone about what he was doing. And the years stretched on without a completed dissertation. He was getting there, but he lacked the kind of interchange that would have helped him, we think, to actually finish.

ADVICE

Now, we've just given you our first bit of advice, and it concerns how to complete a dissertation in a "reasonable" period of time. But advice, even good advice, does not apply equally to all. The brilliant student we just described faced a family crisis before he could finish the dissertation; circumstances forced him to leave school to take over his parents' business. He might have produced the best dissertation ever written in his field, leading to talk, when it was published, that he had worked on it for 15 years and that was why it was so brilliant. His whole reputation might have been enhanced by his slow progress, even though he suffered financially and emotionally during the time he was actually working on it. So here is the second piece of advice: Take our advice and the advice that others give you with a grain of salt.

Of course, there are many kinds of advice. Some advice is specific and directive. Many teachers have said that they like advice about lesson plans, for example, to be complete and clear. They want a lesson plan that they can use in their classrooms. They want the lesson plan to be a recipe. Another kind of advice is less directive. Using the lesson plan metaphor again, the advice might take the form of an idea for a lesson plan. The teacher then would supply the interpretation and application of the idea to a particular situation. This book presents advice in the second manner. Our advice will be in the form of ideas rather than recipes.

Also, advice is never neutral. People who give advice always have a particular stake in it. They may have a particular set of values they want to uphold or a desire for you to see them in specific ways. The stakes may serve your interests, or not. Sometimes you will get conflicting advice from different faculty members whom you admire. When this happens, try to figure out what their investments are. Are they promoting a particular theoretical view they want you to employ? Are they pushing you to finish quickly so you can be competitive for jobs or research grants? Do they have an investment in the topic? Are department, college, or national politics involved? There is no right or wrong answer to these questions, but the more you know about the stake that the advice giver has in the advice, the better you will be able to evaluate the advice.

Our original point was that there are many people for you to turn to on campus for help with your work. So why do we write this book? We write it particularly for doctoral students who are writing qualitative dissertations and who are looking for some ways to think about the problems they face. As with any research, writing a dissertation—in addition to choosing a topic, collecting data, and figuring out what to say—involves making many choices. And the choices you make will affect the other work you have done. You can enhance the data you have collected, or not. You can make your topic seem important to others, or not. And so on. This is a book that we hope will help you to figure out what you should be thinking about when you are making some of these choices. It is a book that contains advice, but the advice is less important than the frames we offer for ways of thinking about these choices. This is because often there are a number of good choices you can make, but you want to consider these choices in a thoughtful way that will serve your goals.

As we describe situations we will offer examples. The experiences will be real, as will the names associated with them. If there are no names connected to the examples, it means that we are preserving the anonymity of our informants.

One of the fundamental characteristics of qualitative research is that it always studies the process of meaning making in context. In fact, Eliot Mischler (1979) titled one of his articles, "Meaning in Context: Is There Any Other Kind?" When we write a qualitative dissertation, the context in which you produce it is as significant as the topic you write about. There are multiple environments for doing this kind of work, and they shape the process. If your department is located at a school that has a critical mass of qualitative researchers who are fluent with methodological issues, then you have the most supportive environment for doing your work because you do not have to argue for the worth or value of the method. If your department or college is primarily quantitative, then you will have the added responsibility of having to explain the function and value of the approach and you will have to resist the temptation to be on the defensive. And then there are many areas of middle ground. We will discuss these concerns more fully in Chapter 3.

WHAT IS A QUALITATIVE DISSERTATION?

The qualitative dissertation can take many forms. We have an idea in mind when we talk about the qualitative dissertation, but you don't have to have that same idea. When we talk about the qualitative dissertation, we imagine a document that has seven chapters: the introduction, literature review, methods and procedures, three data chapters, and the conclusion. The project in the qualitative dissertation that we imagine was originally posed as an open-ended question whose goal was to explore the perspectives of a particular set of informants on their experiences. These informants might have been part of a project to study a person or a group, so that the question is exploring how an individual, a series of individuals, or a particular group makes sense of their lives. Possible questions for dissertation projects would look something like the following: What are the perspectives of high school students who participate in an early morning discussion group on social issues? How do women who are college students understand what it means to be feminine, and how do they prepare themselves to be seen in public as feminine? How do people with hepatitis C understand the meaning of their disease? How do pregnant and parenting teens experience sex education? How do people who are married to or partnered with people in the defense industry understand militarism? (see Riley, 2000). Another kind of focus for a qualitative dissertation might be a process. So these kinds of questions would examine how ideas shift over time: How do students get through 4 years of high school? What strategies do African American women develop to successfully complete college at a predominantly White campus?

Yet another focus for a dissertation can be on social relations—that is, the power differentials between different social groups. A dissertation question with this kind of focus might explore the power struggles between a disability rights group and a campus administration. Finally, a qualitative dissertation as we describe it might look at an event like 9/11, the blackout that hit the Northeast in 2003, or the SARS epidemic. How did graduate students from Kuwait, Saudi Arabia, and Jordan experience life on an American campus after 9/11? How do college administrators understand the idea of "threat"? We have phrased these questions to emphasize the idea of perspective and the focus on the meaning-making process. The actual dissertation titles would not necessarily be the same as these questions.

Some dissertations explore the perspectives of a particular group in a single setting, while others look at the perspectives of a certain kind of group across several settings. Some dissertations are framed as case studies, while others are organized to build theory by exploring ideas across settings. However the questions were originally framed, the researcher narrows the focus after collecting data for a while. You may decide that in spite of the original plans, more data are necessary, making it imperative to return to the field. Or, after doing some research, you might decide that you need to change the way you framed the dissertation, perhaps by adding a historical chapter or by removing one. You do not design your study in the qualitative approach and then carry out the work. Design is more mobile than this and requires some flexibility. Dissertations can be more descriptive or more analytical. Whatever end of the spectrum they are on, they argue points (we will discuss more about the nature of an argument in Chapter 2), which they illustrate with examples from the data. So they are presented in predominantly narrative form, though they may utilize charts as well.

The kind of qualitative dissertation we imagine is interpretive, rooted in what is called the Chicago School approach. A group of sociologists under the original leadership of Robert Park, a former journalist, formed the sociology department at the University of Chicago during the 1920s and 1930s, and they studied different aspects of community life. They studied the work of real estate agents, waitresses, homeless people—the perspectives of people in all walks of life. They studied different communities, including richer and poorer areas, and tried to examine the relationship between the perspectives of individual people and the environments or contexts in which they lived. In this approach, informants hold interest for researchers not so much as individuals but as representatives of particular groups. From this approach to qualitative research, many wider and differently named ways of doing this sort of scholarship have developed.

Many of these approaches build on the relationship of biography and social structure (Mills, 1959). You may be interested in conducting an institutional ethnography so that you can look at power relations around a particular issue (Campbell & Gregor, 2004; Smith, 2005). Or you may want to use feminist methods to study your topic so that you can respect the experiences of your informants in particular ways, approach the lives of women as central rather than as peripheral to human experience, and make the social location of the researcher part of the text (see DeVault, 1999, for an expansive discussion of these issues). You may want to use critical race theory to study questions of race and racism in American society. Critical race theory understands racism as a normal part of our culture and emphasizes the importance of people of color narrating their stories (see, for example, Duncan, 2002; Ladson-Billings, 2003; Solorzano & Yosso, 2002). All of these examples represent interpretive projects.

Some qualitative methods take more structured forms than we have described. You may prepare open-ended survey questions that demand narrative responses and consider this work qualitative. This approach, in fact, is the form that many departments understand qualitative research to take. Or you may develop an observation guide to explore the ways students in college composition classes discuss race, where the same observations are made in six classrooms. This kind of approach is also considered qualitative because it produces narrative data. There is also the sense in both of these forms—the open-ended survey and the structured observation—that no matter how definite the plans are ahead of time, the work could go in a different direction.

Many students are currently attracted to another approach that they want to consider qualitative. They might call it *qualitative content analysis*. This approach involves recording and analyzing various forms of print or visual texts to see how they handle particular issues. Topics might include how girls are represented in teen advice columns, how sitcoms take up race, or how Arab peoples are represented in *National Geographic*. In order to be considered qualitative, however, any kind of textual analysis must also include the perspectives of some audience, so that in addition to analyzing text, the researcher also interviews the magazine readers or writers, the television viewers, or the moviegoers. Researchers may show films to students in focus groups and record how the students talk about the films. Or they can analyze how teen magazines represent girls in their advice columns and also interview readers of these columns. They can look at dialogue in chat rooms, but they also have to interview (perhaps via e-mail) some of the participants (see Johns, Chen, & Hall, 2004). It is necessary to include the interpretive part of the research because qualitative researchers are interested in texts that are in use.

WHO DO WE IMAGINE YOU ARE?

Whenever you write, you write for an audience. An audience contains the people who will read your text. A thoughtful writer imagines the characteristics or nature of a particular audience and keeps this mental image in mind when writing. For this text, for example, we imagine a group of people who, no matter what their other talents or interests, need and plan to write a dissertation. You are either full- or part-time students at a university, and you plan to use qualitative methods to do your research. You have different levels of support from your institution for this kind of work, and you are looking to get some outside advice.

When you write a dissertation, even though you might be hoping or planning to publish it, you write for the audience of your dissertation committee. This is your primary audience because these are the people who will make the official judgment about the acceptability of your research. Dissertation committees have particular expectations of dissertation research because these committees act like an oversight panel. They judge whether or not you have "passed muster" to become certified to be a nonmedical doctor. So, simply put, if you write your dissertation knowing that your dissertation committee is your audience, you have a better chance of communicating what you want to this group and a better chance of having them interpret your perspectives in the way that you intend.

If it were this simple, however, we could give such straightforward advice, and you could choose whether or not to follow it. But the task is more complicated than this. Sometimes, while you must write for your dissertation committee, you also are writing for other audiences, and you feel that you must include those readers as well. Let's say, for example, that you are a person of color, and your dissertation is on college students' perspectives on hip-hop culture. You feel that you are not just writing for your dissertation committee but that you are also ethically impelled to frame how people perform race in American culture in a manner that honors Black cultural experiences as well as the power of institutional racism. If you have selected a dissertation committee that respects your views and understands your theoretical orientation, then you actually *are* writing for your committee. But many students in this situation feel that they are writing for their communities as well, and they think that they must take their communities into account. This is an important consideration, and dissertation committees must also take this into account.

WHAT THIS BOOK IS

This book takes you through the process of producing a good dissertation. As we said earlier, it does not teach you how to do qualitative research. But it addresses many of the issues that may arise as you work towards the completed—and defended—dissertation. Chapter 2 addresses the question: What makes a good dissertation? It describes award-winning dissertations and discusses some of the important considerations in doing good work. Chapter 3 looks at dissertation advisors and dissertation committees, emphasizing the significance of good relationships and portraying methods of communication and expectations. Chapter 4 addresses the protection of human subjects, focusing particularly on how the candidate gets approval from Institutional Review Boards that must approve research with human subjects. Chapter 5 concerns the qualitative proposal, considering when it should be written, what it should look like, and what purpose it serves. Chapter 6 goes through all of the chapters of the qualitative dissertation, describing what the expectations are for them and what you might confront as you write them. In Chapter 7, we consider the writing process, looking at writing as a kind of work. We look at different styles of completing this work and discuss strategies for managing the difficulties. In Chapter 8 we get to the defense of the dissertation. In the description and analysis of this event, we hope that familiarity with the process will alleviate your anxiety. Chapter 9 takes a brief look at the nontraditional qualitative dissertation.

This book does not take a recipe-for-success approach to the dissertation. Neither is it solely theoretical. It is a modest, practical book that we hope you will find useful in the process of starting and completing a good qualitative dissertation.

CHAPTER 2

What Makes a Good Dissertation?

Some dissertation writers just want to finish the project and move on. They're just doing it for some form of certification and don't think of themselves as scholars. But most doctoral students want to write a good dissertation. It would be nice if there were a formula that advisors could give their students to guarantee a good dissertation, but, as you—and we—know, there isn't. A great idea can sometimes become a mediocre dissertation, and a narrowly conceived project can sometimes turn out well. It depends on many factors, including the approach you take to the topic (the angle), the writing, how it is put together, and the timeliness of the topic, among other things. There is no formula because the story you tell (and how you choose to tell it) makes a difference for the final product and sometimes renders predictions impossible.

At this point, it may sound like we are saying, "It's all up to you. Pull yourself up by your bootstraps. You can make it or break it." We do not take this point of view. Your part in this project is obviously central. Thoughtfulness, hard work, good field relations when you're collecting data—these are just a few of the aspects of the project that are up to you. But your environment makes a big difference. Your facility with qualitative approaches, the kind of training you have had as a qualitative researcher, a supportive community, and the level of sophistication that dialogue with others fosters are all important factors in the dissertation process. Look at dissertations that are published by leading publishers or that win awards (see the Resource Guide for examples of published dissertations). The acknowledgment section in their books is usually filled with multiple thank-yous to leading scholars in the field who advised the author and helped in the dissertation production process and to others "who were there for me." A dissertation is rarely an individual project. But the process of getting a doctorate is often constructed as if it were a test that an individual has to pass; so doctoral students often end up feeling that they are always working to pass a test. Students often say that this feeling drains energy from them, making them feel like they are always trying to live up to some test results or standards that they cannot describe. Try to avoid this trap. Do work that you believe in and that you think is important, and seek guidance and help as you need it. A dissertation is not Mt. Everest.

In this chapter we address the question of what a good dissertation looks like. We consider the relationship between a good dissertation and the kinds of ideas that frequently lead to good dissertations. We distinguish between approaches that negotiate topics and ideas with their informants, so that the study cannot be completely worked out ahead of time, and those that simply use informants' words to illustrate a predetermined topic. We pay some attention to the interdisciplinary dissertation since recently there has been greater interest in interdisciplinary work. We describe different strategies to gain narrative authority (since you will be the narrator of your dissertation), and, finally, we address the question of the argument.

Can we really define "good"? Yes. But we want to hold off on this definition for a moment to look at the stories of three dissertation writers. We describe their work and then look at the similarities and differences between them.

THREE DISSERTATIONS AND THEIR GENESIS

Ronnie

Ronnie was interested in studying educational travel. He liked to travel, and he was interested in what people thought they could learn from going to other countries and in how companies planned and promoted educational travel. He did some preliminary work on the topic. He got a copy of a magazine called *The Sophisticated Traveler* and wrote letters to all the companies advertising educational travel in the magazine to ask for copies of their brochures. He found a small educational travel company that sponsored different kinds of educational travel and ecotourism. Through this company, he traveled to one of the places that taught Spanish while students lived in another country. In addition, he decided that he would approach the topic from multiple points of view. One aspect of the study would include the perspectives of educational travelers who went on trips offered by the company. Another aspect would examine the content of the brochures that advertisers used to recruit travelers by means of interviews with some of the companies that produced these brochures. As he was working on these topics, he began to feel that the history of educational travel was significant and was a project that had not been adequately addressed in the literature. So he decided that, in addition to doing historical secondary research on the history of educational travel, he would frame one chapter historically and analyze some archival documents on travel. He thought that if he could show how this particular trip was, in fact, educational, this categorization would help him to define educational travel. He produced a dissertation that included qualitative interviews, historical analysis, and textual analysis combined with interviews with the producers of the brochures (Casella, 1997).

Lesley

Initially, Lesley wanted to study some issue connected to youth, schooling, and popular culture—the title of a course for which she had first been the teaching assistant and then had taught on her own. What kind of topic would bring these three concerns together? She heard about a group of high school kids from one of the local city high schools that met every Wednesday morning before school in a church near the high school campus. These students wanted to discuss current issues, to talk about the schooling process, and to be political and relevant in a way that they thought they could not in their classes. She got permission from the kids to study them and attended their group meetings once a week for about 2½ years. Her dissertation ended up addressing several questions. First, she devoted one chapter to the idea that although the students thought of themselves as social critics, they ended up replicating many social values that confirmed the status quo. She also examined how this group understood what it meant to be cool as well as how the boys and girls in the group experienced coolness quite differently. Finally, she wrote about how the kids both criticized and benefited from their education, looking at what they took for granted in their analysis of schooling. Her informants were youths, the topic of popular culture was connected to her analysis of coolness, and she devoted a chapter to students' talk of schooling and their social location in relation to that talk (Bogad, 2002).

Brenda

Brenda had been a social worker and was getting her doctorate in sociology. She was interested in the relationship between a new welfare policy that changed the formula to provide aid to women with young children and the everyday experiences of the women in these new programs. She decided to focus on the new welfare-to-work policies, and she heard about a training program for nursing aides that would occur not too far from her home. She received permission from the director of the program and the teacher in it to follow several groups of students through their coursework and fieldwork. She hung out with the nursing aides in class, took some of the tests with them, went with them on their coffee breaks, and, later, visited the nursing homes with the women when they had their practicum experiences. Her dissertation examined how women who had once been on welfare became the working poor. She looked at the relationship between the kinds of work that these women did at home and in the nursing homes, at how caring for people is professionally taught, and at how the relationships that developed between the women in the program ended up supporting them. Institutional ethnography theoretically informed her work (Solomon, 1999).

In all of these cases, the students started with broad topics and with clear ideas about what they were interested in, but they were unaware of how the dissertation would address the questions. In time, that would emerge from fieldwork, the data gathered, and the way the researcher (with advice from an adviser) would come to think about the meaning of the data. Ronnie used multiple methods to cut a broad swath through the field of educational travel. Lesley employed participant observation and in-depth interviewing for a case study of a single group of high school students involved in an informal extracurricular activity. Brenda studied the relationship between "national policy and situated meaning" (Bogdan, 1976) through a study of a single site, also using participant observation and interviewing, but with three sets of informants. All three dissertations won awards, yet they took quite different approaches.

THE QUALITIES OF A GOOD DISSERTATION

Can we really define the good dissertation? A good dissertation, like any qualitative data, does not have meaning in and of itself. Just as the meanings of qualitative data are not transparent, the good dissertation is good because the readers who interact with it think it is good. Evaluations of quality are interactive. A committee might think a dissertation is good because it adds new information, provides an interesting perspective on a subject, proposes a new approach to a topic, offers a sophisticated analysis of an issue, presents rich descriptions of a group that has never been studied, is extremely well written, expands a field of study, and so forth.

A Broad Question

What did these three researchers have in common? First, they all started with a broad question about a topic that was of great interest to them, and they worked to make it interesting and notable to the reader. The significance of the broad question is that it permits a kind of dialogue between the researcher and the topic. The researcher has a particular interest in a set of issues that he or she thinks is important to explore, and the site has a particular dynamic. The researcher learns from the "first days in the field" (Geer, 1964) what the important questions are to the informants. The dialogue is what takes place between the researcher's original idea in entering the field and the informants' understanding of their situation.

A broad topic is also useful because, ironically, it usually allows the researcher to get into a meaty situation early on. Many new researchers think that a narrow question will help them not to waste time on too many irrelevant ideas, but, actually, narrow questions usually make it more difficult for the research to proceed because the informants may not conceptualize the problem as the researcher does, and so the researcher thinks that "there is nothing here."

Rich Data

Second, all of these researchers collected rich data, that is, detailed observations about what they observed and interview transcripts that forced informants to be specific. The data are the evidence, and rich data that provide specific examples about how the informants understand their situations and how they make sense of things are crucial to making a case, involving the readers, and offering some depth. Without rich data, the reader can only assume that you are leaping to your conclusion. Here is an example of a discussion that took place recently in a dissertation defense. A student wrote a dissertation on how play therapists understand children. She was interested in what play therapists called on in their training, in their reading, and in the predominant social values they used to make sense of what a child was, since it was clear to her that this didn't just come from observation alone. These therapists drew on particular discourses or social ideas to make sense of what a kid is. In the discussion, one of the examiners asked the doctoral candidate to offer evidence for her statement that play therapists want to be "healers" of children—that is, to get to what they described as the "root" of the problem—rather than to be "fixers." Play therapists condemned fixers as people who wanted the symptoms of the problem "to go away" without addressing the cause of the problem. Because the candidate had collected detailed accounts of the therapists' perspectives, she was able to offer numerous examples from her data to support her argument and to revise the dissertation later to make the evidence for her claims more explicit.

Knowledge of Informants

Third, each of the doctoral students knew their informants well. They had spent significant time with them—in the case of the high school discussion group, the researcher spent almost 2½ years with the group—and were able to interpret their informants' meanings in the context in which they were made. The researchers did not visualize their informants' words as "responses" to questions, as text that had meaning in and of itself. Rather, they saw that when their informants said or did things, part of the meaning of the words related to their being in a particular situation. Their task was to see the meanings in context. The researchers understood that when their informants spoke, they were in some ways conscious of the situations they were in: The informants spoke in interviews, in group meetings, in focus groups, or in class, and the specific nature of the context made a difference. But, because the researchers had studied their informants over time, they saw how they responded in specific situations. The high school students were affected differently by where the researcher saw them: in their discussion group, in individual interviews, riding in the researcher's car after the meeting on the way to school, or in the public school events where the researcher also observed them.

The researchers also thought about the social and physical contexts of their informants' lives. Lesley's study of the morning discussion group examined the urban high school that the students attended as part of the context as well as the media's promotion of our "postfeminist" age. Brenda pointed to federal policies about welfare reform as the context for shaping the changes in her informants' lives.

Good Writing

Fourth, the dissertations were well written. The researchers paid attention to the mechanics and style of writing, and they drew readers in. The writers were aware of their audience. Good writing can take many different forms. Some writers are spare, not loading their sentences with too many adjectives or metaphors. Since metaphors are often overused and hence stripped of meaning, they do not convey as much meaning as the writer might like. Others try to capture the richness of data by writing dense description. Both can work. We will attend to issues of writing and writing style in Chapter 7.

Analysis of the Data

Fifth, the doctoral students developed analyses of their data. They did not act as if the data spoke for themselves, as if meanings were transparent.

Rather, they interpreted what the data meant. They acted as guides through the data, explained why they made particular interpretations, and related these conclusions to the literature or to theory.

Social Location

Also, the writers all described their own relationship to the data and the idea. Sometimes this is referred to as the researcher's "social location." One's social location means particular identity markers (like race, class, or gender), circumstances of one's individual situation, and other things in relation to the informants. The reader needs to know the criteria you used to decide what to put into the dissertation and why you focused on what you did. Explaining your relationship to the data and the idea shows the reader your awareness of some of the lenses that filtered how you "saw" people, events, and issues in your study, and helps the reader to judge your relationship to the data and your analysis.

Theorize About Meaning

Finally, the writers theorized about meaning. This means that they looked at the social values embedded in the issues that their informants raised and the descriptions they offered. It means that they wrote about the shared ideas that were referred to when their informants used certain language or vocabulary. For her dissertation on technology in schools, Dara collected data on teachers' uses of technology in different fields. The principal made some resources, but not others, available to teachers. In her analysis of these choices, Dara looked at what the principal took for granted about what the schoolday should look like (Wexler, 2003).

COMING UP WITH AN IDEA FOR THE DISSERTATION

What should you write a dissertation about? People make all kinds of statements about the topic. Some say you should be passionate about it because the dissertation demands so much work and you will be working on it for a while. Or people will say that "there is a big gap in the literature, so this is a great topic." Another frequently heard bit of advice is, "Write on a 'hot' topic, because then you will be able to publish from it more easily." There is certainly truth in all of these statements. You should definitely feel passion for your topic, it is useful if you can fill a gap in the literature or offer a different take on a topic, and it is always helpful if the topic you're enthusiastic about is of interest to others. But how do you come up with a topic?

When one of us (Sari) was ready to do a dissertation, she knew that she was interested in writing something about women and education. But she did not know how to frame a study. Which piece of this huge topic should she investigate? There was no qualitative methods class offered at her graduate school, and her research methods professor seemed somewhat hostile to both her interest in research on women and her desire to do qualitative research. She decided that she needed to go elsewhere to get some advice. Seymour Sarason, a professor at Yale University, was a friend, and over dinner this experienced researcher broke the big issue—something to do with women and education—into seven or eight ways to do a dissertation on this topic. The author chose one of them—the perspectives that adult women hold on their experience as girls in elementary school—and wrote her dissertation about these perspectives and the discourses that shaped the informants' talk. The most impressive aspect of this dinner was that Sarason could take a broad idea and develop so many different ways of investigating it. The message is that experience doing research, an interest in methods, and having an imagination enables you to develop multiple ways of thinking about a topic.

When you imagine a topic for yourself, it is always useful to first think of several ways of approaching it so that you have a choice about what to do. Having choices is always better than just "falling into" a topic because you are specifically choosing it. In workshops or classes we often ask a student to volunteer a topic he or she is considering and work to get the group to imagine multiple ways of approaching the study. Sometimes this idea of considering a topic from multiple vantage points works well because it enables you to choose the perspective that most interests you and the particular issues that you want to address. If you're interested in bilingual education, for example, do you want to look at it from the perspective of the students? Teachers? Parents? Do you want to do a case study where you consider how all of these perspectives, and perhaps those of school administrators and district officials as well, are part of the mix? Or are you more interested in doing an institutional ethnography where you examine how discourses that circulate about immigrants get embedded in state policies and emerge in the ways that teachers talk about their work as bilingual teachers? Perhaps you would like to follow a group of young kids who enter school as bilingual speakers through their years in junior high school to see what happens to them. Or you might want to study a group of students who enter an elementary school not speaking English well, observe them becoming bilingual, and shadow them in their classes and their neighborhood.

Clearly there are many ways to approach this topic, and thinking through your choices is one way of categorizing your interests and the choices that you might have. But this is not the only way to decide on a topic. Sometimes you do not really decide until you have started your research. Then something happens in the field that makes you take notice. Let's look at a different approach to framing a study.

As you imagine framing the study, the question arises of what story you will tell. Here we use another example to illustrate a different way that a specific topic can emerge. Say you decide that you want to study the reaction of high school students and teachers to the *Challenger* disaster. You are particularly interested in how educators and their students understand the value and danger of such flights. You wonder how teachers and students think about the educational implications of the *Challenger* disaster. You interview teachers and students individually and in focus groups, finding that the informants say much the same thing whether other people are present or not. You had considered whether there might be contradictions between the more public and personal reflections. A strong finding across all the groups was that informants worried about the impact of Christa McAuliffe's death on her children. They spoke about their concerns in significant detail and with great feeling. The informants did not all share the same views on her role, but they all raised this question about the effect of McAuliffe's death on her family. They did not raise the same concern about the death of the male astronauts. You begin to wonder if people think differently about motherless and fatherless children. You first decide that one chapter will explore the informants' perspectives on gender and space flight, specifically concerns about women astronauts with young children. But the more you work with your data, the closer you come to deciding that even though you were not particularly interested in gender when you started, given the way your data are shaping up, gender seems the most interesting aspect of your research. So you decide to focus on gender. You need to do more interviewing now that you have narrowed your topic in a different way from your earliest expectations. One theme explores the issue of motherless and fatherless children in our culture as the discussion of space flight disasters evoked it. Another theme examines what it means to be a "male astronaut" and a "female astronaut." And your third theme will explore what language is available for talking about gender, emotions, and major public events. This "new" dissertation looks different from what you originally expected your work to cover, but it is closely connected to the kinds of talk that you heard from the high school students and teachers you interviewed.

DOING AN INTERDISCIPLINARY DISSERTATION

Having an interdisciplinary background and research agenda is much valued in the social sciences. There are well-known journals that are geared to an interdisciplinary approach, faculty job announcements that state preferences for candidates with interdisciplinary backgrounds, and books and articles considered "classics" that achieved this status through the author's interdisciplinary work. Before discussing the ins and outs of writing an interdisciplinary dissertation, we define what is meant by *interdisciplinary*. In a general sense, doing interdisciplinary work means that the author who is studying in a particular field—let's say social work—is also using the insights, theories, literature, and research strategies that are used in other fields that are not often associated with social work. A doctoral candidate in social work at an Ivy League university described what she meant when she talked about her interdisciplinary dissertation, which was a study of public housing architecture:

> I study social work—that's the school I am in. But when I first started studying housing, which is my subfield, I found that some of the most interesting work on housing was being done not by social workers but by cultural geographers, people in communications, and others who were examining the broader cultural and geopolitical constructions of what housing tells us about policy, not so much how policy affects housing, which is the traditional way of scholarship in schools of social work such as mine.

When choosing to do an interdisciplinary dissertation, the first step is to be able to articulate why an interdisciplinary dissertation is necessary. Why is it important that your topic be examined by using the knowledge, literature, and methods of a field that is not your own? Interdisciplinary work can pose a challenge to dissertation committee members who do not know, and sometimes do not appreciate, the work in other fields that you may find necessary to incorporate. You should explain why it is important that you are studying, for example, popular magazines when your field is education: You can think of it as the "significance" part of your dissertation. In this case, when you are stating the significance of your dissertation, which is a mainstay of a proposal or introductory chapter in a dissertation, not only will you state the importance of your topic but you will also state the importance of studying the topic in the way you intend. Here you should very clearly state the significance of the interdisciplinary work as if you were writing for the most discipline-based individuals in your department. Following are some pointers you could keep in the back of your mind as you develop your proposal and work through the first draft of your dissertation.

- Your interdisciplinary work should demonstrate the value of interdisciplinary analyses. You want to be able to highlight why your dissertation is distinctive and significant because of its interdisciplinary nature. You need to be able to answer the question: Why is your interdisciplinary method important to the overall dissertation?

- You need to be willing to gain much knowledge outside your field. This should include taking doctoral-level classes in fields that are not your own. Your literature review will need to encompass more than your field and will often be longer and more far-ranging than the traditional literature review.
- Your dissertation committee should represent the different fields you are involved in. You must be able to find professors outside your field who are willing to be a part of a dissertation committee outside their schools, sometimes with other professors they do not know.
- You should be prepared to submit to journals outside your field and to attend conferences that are not ordinarily attended by those in your field. In order to have more than a superficial knowledge of the various fields you are incorporating into your dissertation, you should immerse yourself in the other fields as if you were truly a part of them, not just borrowing from them.

There are also some cautionary notes involved in the doing of an interdisciplinary dissertation. They include the following:

- Though you may understand the importance of interdisciplinary work, not all people do. This can affect your dissertation and career in several ways. For example, in fields that are traditional, it may be difficult to find a university position if your work does not "fit inside the box."
- Related to the first point, it is possible that an Institutional Review Board may have difficulty approving your research. In some cases, they may not be accustomed to the research method and may not know how to respond. Others may feel threatened by it because the interdisciplinary method does not conform to traditional research strategies, although this perspective is rare these days.
- Regarding dissertation committees, power plays can arise when professors are from different departments and sometimes different schools within a university. For example, there is a hierarchy of fields that can cause tensions when students of education or social work involve professors from outside fields, especially when those fields are more respected or considered more scholarly than education or social work.
- Pragmatic concerns can arise related to schedules and distances between individuals in different schools and sometimes different

universities in different parts of the country. When doing inter-disciplinary work, one does not often have the luxury of having a close-knit group of professors within a single field (and univer-sity department) who know each other and are probably used to working with each other.

Of course, these cautionary notes do not apply in all circumstances. Although it might be difficult to find a university position when your work is not traditional, you might have a better chance of landing a job when universities are seeking interdisciplinary faculty members. Each dissertation writer will have to determine how pertinent these potential problems are. But there are several steps that can be followed not only to avoid some of the pitfalls of interdisciplinary work but also to capitalize on its benefits.

Step 1. Be able to articulate in a proposal and in everyday corridor and classroom discussions why your interdisciplinary work is impor-tant to your field in particular and the social sciences in general.

Step 2. Nurture good relationships with professors outside your field who are known for their interdisciplinary work. This can be done by taking classes with the professors or arranging for indepen-dent studies with them (which can be done with professors in other universities).

Step 3. Through classes, independent studies, conferences, and your literature review, attempt to become proficient in the ideas, major figures, theories, topics, and research methods of each of the fields you are incorporating into your work. Keep your knowl-edge current.

Step 4. Find other research, including dissertations that are similar to your own. Use these as models, but also develop your disserta-tion so that it furthers the knowledge and analyses presented in this other research.

Step 5. Develop a working group of individuals who are doing simi-lar interdisciplinary work. This can include individuals in your own school and department as well as individuals across the coun-try. Locally, this may take the form of a reading group; a support-ive group of like-minded people at a distance can be maintained through e-mail and other forms of electronic communication, con-ferences, joint projects, and other venues.

Step 6. Prepare yourself for a lifetime of creative and discipline-stretching research of the sort many scholars find the most inter-esting and revealing. Also prepare yourself for possible pitfalls such as those discussed earlier.

In many ways, doing an interdisciplinary dissertation is similar to doing a dissertation that conforms to the expectations of a single discipline. However, there are issues that can arise when doing an interdisciplinary dissertation that should be considered. This section tried to cover some of the concerns, but the extent to which these will affect you depends on your predicament, field, department, and career choices.

NARRATIVE AUTHORITY

What Is Narrative Authority?

Narrative authority means that the reader of a qualitative study believes the text's narrator or sees the narrator as believable; this authority is important because it is a source of power in your relationship with readers. The narrator can write against the reader's common sense, can take a point of view that challenges a reader's deeply held beliefs, or can even reaffirm what the reader already knows. Whatever the strategy or strategies used to gain authority, some of which we address here, the narrative cannot have authority outside of a relationship with the reading audience.

We might expect narrative authority in the qualitative study to be independent of fashion and fad. But narrative authority is very much related to cultural currency because we are talking about writing for a public. And publics have ideas about what is in style or what is important for this historical moment. Certain kinds of narrative styles and particular representations of the field carry currency at different historical moments, and these must be taken into account when discussing authority.

It is more important now than ever before, for example, for narrators of qualitative studies to describe their own cultural and social locations, to discuss their personal experiences in the field, to communicate to readers what about themselves is relevant to a particular project in order to counteract the "view from nowhere" kind of science writing (see Haraway, 1991). Although writing with a presence counters this objectifying view that the omniscient narrator represents, telling readers things about yourself—your emotions, failings, and so on—does not necessarily improve your study, your findings, or the significance of your project. To use Van Maanen's (1988) vocabulary here, the "confessional" or "impressionist" narrator does not necessarily have greater authority or believability than the realist one. Always ask yourself what difference it will make for the reader to know personal things about you. Telling things about yourself to your audience is a narrative strategy that may work at particular times to help you gain authority with readers. There are ways of doing studies that make one better than another, but there need to be multiple forms of quality.

While we may associate authority with authoritarianism or patriarchy (since *patriarchal authority* is a common phrase), authority takes many forms, including casual and assertive, direct and indirect. As dissertation writers, you also need to establish narrative authority, as mentioned earlier. You need to show your readers, specifically your dissertation committee, that you have a certain authority to speak about your subject. In this next section we offer you some resources to draw on for establishing narrative authority.

The six narrative strategies that we describe include physicality, temporality, theory, rhetoric, authentication, and timeliness.

Physicality and Temporality

"Being there" is central to the qualitative approach. Qualitative methodologists spend significant time in the field, and this time makes their work more than just a series of impressions. Narrators who can effectively communicate how experience with informants over a significant period of time benefited their research gain authority. What makes your approach effective is how it demonstrates your continuity in the field and your account's dependence on the time you spent there. This means that you need to show that someone who participated in "blitzkrieg ethnography" (Rist, 1980) would not have the same depth of understanding that you do. It means that you need to demonstrate an intimate familiarity with the lives of your informants or the geographic site where you observed. You should not just know your informants' views on things; you should know how their views relate to their lives. There are many collections that discuss fieldwork, and you can take advantage of these for examples (e.g., Lareau & Shultz, 1996; Watson, 1999; Wolf, 1996). You do not need to put all your knowledge in the methods section; in fact, you probably could not contain it there.

Certain ways of narrating your data emphasize physicality and temporality. Some examples show how you can create some authority without directly addressing it:

> Jennifer walked into the classroom, dressed in her usual outfit of black pants and a colorful shirt. Sometimes the shirt was magenta or emerald. Today's choice was pumpkin.

These small details communicate knowledge over time.

> Jack Johnson blew the whistle, and began his after-game routine. He gathered the soccer team together under the oak tree at the corner

of the playground, turned to the captain first, and asked for her take on the day's plays. "How d'ya think it went today, Jen?" he asked. He listened to her comments, nodding his head now and then, looking at her the entire time. When she finished, it was silent for a while. Then, as he always did, he looked around the group and said, "OK, gang. What do the rest of you think?" Since most of the players generally wanted to say something, their hands would fly up. Today, he called on Bernice first, pointing his finger at her and saying, "Bern?"

Using the phrase *as he always did* and referring to players who *generally are* anxious to talk shows your familiarity with a setting over time.

This narrative form is not a sophisticated strategy, but it is effective because it shows rather than announces your authority.

Theoretical Sophistication

Although important, "being there" is not enough. One's orientation, values, subject position, and identities influence what you see and how you interpret the meanings that you argue your informants make. You also gain narrative authority through the thoughtfulness with which you can describe those theories that explain your perspectives on your subjects and that account for how you see the world.

Rhetoric

Narrators can gain authority through their rhetoric. By rhetoric, we mean "the putting to work of language in order to influence other people, either in terms of their future actions or their beliefs" (Edgar & Sedgwick, 1999, p. 340). Tropes, or figures of speech, that authors use are part of a piece's rhetoric. Another part can be the style of language. And still another aspect can be the portrait you construct for the reader of your learning the culture you study. Doug Foley (1990) gained authority by representing himself in *Learning Capitalist Culture* as at home with his informants. The researcher felt at home and could rely on knowledge from his childhood experiences to develop rapport. He collapsed differences between these different time periods (his youth and the time of his fieldwork) to represent his comfort in rural surroundings and privilege his view as narrator. Annette Lareau (1989), in *Home Advantage*, her study of schooling and social class, gained authority by showing not how much she already knew about school systems but by writing about how much she had to learn. This description of her vulnerability also established her authority. It showed that she was confident enough to share her mistakes and lack of clarity because the work she produced demonstrated how she successfully worked through the problems. She also contributed to helping others work through problems by showing how fieldwork always involves shifting grounds. Clearly, there may be some gendered strategies at work here, with women showing vulnerability and men demonstrating competence, but there is the inverse as well in other examples. So narrators can gain authority when they describe not only their effectiveness but also their errors. The reader can come to know narrators as analysts in this way and gain more trust for them.

This narrative strategy says: You can trust me. I'll show you my weaknesses as well as my strengths, my failings as well as my successes. You'll get the whole picture. I'm not covering anything up. You'll know then that you can trust me. This is an alternative way of being authoritative, and its strengths are sometimes overlooked. The issue is, however, that it must be read as a narrative strategy rather than as a signifier of "truth" or the worth of the study.

Authentication

Narrators in ethnographic studies also use strategies to authenticate their particular view of things. Researchers "know" the world they have studied, and narrators work to authenticate for readers why they know these things well. Again, we work to gain the reader's respect for our authority to tell a story a particular way. "Trouble on Memory Lane" (Biklen, 2004), for example, examines one specific authentication strategy that qualitative researchers frequently use when they are studying young people:

> It is a common practice for narrators in ethnographies of youth to describe their own adolescence in relation to the youth they study. Most of the narrators illustrate how these memories increase their access to the youth, their knowledge of the culture, and their abilities to relate to or accurately understand their informants. (p. 716)

This strategy says: Because I used to be one of them, I know them. While the article critiques this use of memory, the strategy is frequently used to authenticate the narrator's authority.

Timeliness

Are you writing on a topic that people want to read about? You gain narrative authority when you tackle issues that are hot, or that you pioneered when others did not, or that catch people's interest. Sometimes timeliness is hard to predict. Sometimes the literature is a good tool to predict the timeliness of an issue, but it can also promote conventional ways of thinking. Discussion with others is an important way to learn about the timeliness of a topic.

MAKING AN ARGUMENT

Every dissertation has to make an argument. Some of you may think of making an argument as being argumentative. But it is not. A dissertation argument may be argumentative in the sense that it advocates for a policy or idea or in the sense that it promotes a particular way of looking at things, but it may also take many other forms that we will discuss in this section. But while you may know what your dissertation is about when you are proposing it and collecting data for it, you may not be so clear after you have collected data and are writing about what your argument is. This is a typical situation. Before we do qualitative research, we may think that our data will lead us toward an argument and, in fact, write the dissertation for us. Data are central for a dissertation not only because they provide the substance of what you will write about but also because they suggest what you "have" or "don't have" to write about. But data do not provide your argument. And every good dissertation needs to state clearly what the dissertation is about so that the readers know what they will be reading, and what your take on the topic is.

An argument is a coherent way of saying what your dissertation speaks to and speaks for. You make arguments from your data and then represent them in writing. The kind of argument has to fit the approach you take and the way you have conceptualized the problem, the data, and the theorizing you want to do. Because research is part of a conversation, the decisions you make about what kind of argument you use depend, partly, on what is going on in your field.

Each chapter makes an argument, and the dissertation, as a whole, has to make an argument. You set the dissertation argument up through what you write in the introduction, and in the conclusion you show how your chapters interconnect and contribute to different aspects of the argument. Arguments are not necessarily argumentative, though they can be if the work is purely rhetorical or conceptual. You could say that when we use the word *argument*, we are really talking about ways of organizing a chapter. We use the word *argument* because we want to emphasize the significance of making a point and of you, the writer, as the visible architect of this point. *Argument* is defined as "discourse intended to persuade; a

coherent series of statements leading from a premise to a conclusion." Even
if your argument is simply about the need for a particular description, when
your description contradicts other descriptions that have previously been
available, it is useful to think of your point as an argument because it forces
you to ask: How does my text fit together and work toward a particular
point?

FORMS OF ARGUMENT

There are many forms of arguments available to organize the chapters and
the whole of your dissertation. You may use different forms in each chapter without any ill effects. In this section we discuss six kinds of effective
arguments that you can use to structure your chapters.

Arguments That Lay Out Categories

In this form of argument, the whole piece you want to discuss is divided
into parts, which are then described and analyzed. Readers must understand each of the parts if they are to understand the whole. In a chapter
on how women teachers handle conflicts in their work, we were interested in how ways of resolving conflicts related to self-regulation (Biklen,
1995). We developed categories to describe the different ways the teachers handled conflicts they faced. These included: "unhappy compliance,"
where teachers went along with the demands of administrators or the
school district because they were afraid of losing their jobs or making
the administration unhappy if they stated their desires more openly; "the
standoff," where the teachers used the strategy of ignoring what they did
not like and were unable to resolve conflicts; "covert resistance," where
teachers refused to go along with district policies or practices but did
not want to openly state their resistance; and "open resistance," where
large groups of teachers refused to cooperate with policies they could not
tolerate.

This example of different forms of teacher resistance is just one sort of
argument you can construct using categories. There are numerous possibilities: categories of education travel, forms of talk about race, strategies
of teaching reading to struggling high school students, forms of racism that
college students recognize, ways doctors categorize parents of premature
babies (Bogdan, Brown, & Foster, 1982). When knowing different types will
help the reader understand your point, this is an effective form of argument to use.

Arguments That Provide Answers to Questions (That You Ask)

You use this argumentative strategy when you want to organize a chapter around a single point. There may be many smaller points that you will have to subsume under this larger question, but the single question focuses the reader's energy and attention around the main point. Why do college women find it difficult to answer direct questions put to them about gender? This is a question that could organize a chapter. Your presentation of data would lead you to answer this question. At the end of the chapter, the reader should be able to understand the four or five reasons that the women struggled with the question. Another question that might organize a chapter or a dissertation would be: Why do teachers with good intentions to empower girls about their bodies in sex education classes continually fail to do so? This approach requires strong evidence and a good question. It can have a powerful impact.

Arguments That Argue for the Worth of a Topic

This approach is particularly effective when the topic has not heretofore been considered worthy of serious study. The dissertation introduction tries to persuade the reader that a topic previously considered too small, insignificant, or even overstudied deserves attention because of its significance. Then the three data chapters make different points about this. Two dissertations that took this approach investigated understudied topics: cheerleaders and the prom. Both saw them as sites for discussing gender, race, and class. One dissertation (Swaminathan, 1997) showed how cheerleading was a different practice depending on the school where students practiced it. At the city school, for example, being a cheerleader meant that students could "be somebody," while at the wealthy suburban school it meant that you were a failed athlete. *Schooling and the Production of Popular Culture: Negotiating Subjectivities at the High School Prom* (Best, 1998) was the first scholarly writing of any kind on the topic of the prom and culture. It became a much more popular topic a few years later when events at proms made headlines (see Best, 2000).

Arguments That Conceptualize a Topic in a Particular Way

Another form of argument insists on a specific approach to a topic. A number of current scholars, for example, emphasize the significance of the disability rights perspective for the study of people with disabilities (e.g.,

Schwartz, 2006). This is a particularly important form of argument when the approach has not been used in your field. If most researchers studying persons with intellectual disabilities, for example, use a developmental or clinical approach, then using a disability rights perspective can offer a contrasting way of understanding issues that may challenge what others take for granted. Nancy Lesko's (2001) work on adolescents was conceptualized in this form, and argued that taking a developmental approach to adolescents was dangerous because it wrote them off as underdeveloped adults. She argued for a social constructionist approach, instead.

Arguments That Foreground a Specific Theoretical Frame

These arguments describe different theoretical positions and suggest that a particular theoretical approach offers insight not otherwise available. You would use this form of argument if your interest lies in how your data advance theory, rather than in how different theories illuminate data. The text has to describe multiple approaches and then settle on one, explaining its significance for the topic. In "K Is Mentally Ill," for example, Dorothy Smith (1990) shows how an analysis of an account of a person's becoming mentally ill diverges radically from other accounts if theorized through institutional ethnography. If you are concerned with advancing critical race theory or intersectionality, your dissertation can employ data to do just that. Banks (2006) used this form to argue that studying the experiences of Black women at American universities expanded and revised Bourdieu's theories about cultural capital (Bourdieu, 1984, 1997). While Bourdieu's framing of cultural capital contributes to explanations of social reproduction, Banks showed how alternative forms of cultural capital contributed to the students' agency as students and helped them overcome their unfamiliarity with university expectations. In this approach, it is important to make sure that the theories fit the data.

Arguments That Construct Multiple Perspectives on a Topic

This form of argument demonstrates oppositional or contrasting ways of considering a topic. In a case study using symbolic interaction, for example, you might argue for the investments that different participants in a single setting have for their claims (e.g., Luschen, 2005). Or using multisite ethnography (Marcus, 1998), you might—as anthropologist Lila Abu-Lughod (2005) did in her study of television in Egypt—make a specific argument about how particular ideas circulate in or between cultures and are interpreted differently in various communities. Or you might explore how practices such as emotional labor, for example, are enacted and evaluated in different settings (Hochschild, 1983). Here the theories of symbolic interactionism or multisite ethnography, unlike in the previous type of argument discussed, animate the argument, but the argument centers on the data rather than the theory.

In short, there are many elements to the good dissertation. In this chapter we have described a few of the "ingredients" to consider when you shape yours. Your goal is to produce a document that teaches readers a different way of considering an area that they may or may not understand well. You want all the work that you do to produce a strong dissertation—the reading, the planning, the data gathering and analysis, the writing and rewriting—to be visible to the reader without telling the reader to notice them.

CHAPTER 3

Dissertation Advisors and Committees

The dissertation committee consists of your advisor and several committee members. The committee's makeup varies according to the policies of the specific department and college. There is usually a core committee of members who play a more substantive role than readers, who are either less involved or not involved at all until the defense. Sometimes, as in the Sociology Department at Syracuse University, two readers serve on the committee with the three core members from the beginning, attending the proposal defense and offering advice there. Sometimes, as in the School of Education at Syracuse University, the two readers are only brought in at the end of the process, after the dissertation has been completed, and they cannot be members of the candidate's own department. You will work more closely with some members of the committee than with others, and you will work particularly closely with your advisor, who is usually the most significant member of your committee—unless you have a difficult relationship with your advisor.

Dissertation committees serve supportive, pedagogical, and gatekeeping functions. The supportive and pedagogical tasks apply to doctoral students. Committee members use support, advice, praise, and critique to help you to write a defendable dissertation. Committee members also carry out gatekeeping responsibilities on behalf of the professoriate, working to assure that only qualified people who have shown that they understand the research process and can effectively carry out a research project are certified by the institution. These goals are sometimes in tension with one another. Depending on the faculty members' view of this process and of the professoriate, the student's journey differs. And, of course, the context of your institution creates differences as well. If your committee members see part of their job as ensuring that the "standards of the university" are upheld, then the expectations will be different than if there is not such a high standard to be upheld. We are not arguing that highly competitive institutions demand better dissertations than those with lesser reputations. In fact, sometimes the opposite is true: Schools that are less burdened with promoting their reputation often let their students do more innovative work.

The vocabulary of qualifications and standards, however, has a history. These ways of thinking have been used in an exclusionary manner to keep particular groups from the same access to degrees that those with skin, gender, and class privileges have had. People of color, students from working-class backgrounds, and women with multiple identity markers have had to face additional hurdles in the doctoral process—not because a professor has told them that they do not qualify for a doctorate but because the students may contest entrenched topics, approaches, and assumptions. Opening up the pool of who may get a doctorate means that some of the people who want to write dissertations have different ideas from current professors about what topics are significant, what approaches best facilitate an analysis of the problems, and what style of work attracts them. Students who use critical race theory, for example, may be particularly attracted to a discursive narrative style or to particular forms of autoethnography that faculty members are not knowledgeable about. Qualitative methods, however, are particularly flexible, and they have a history in the United States of use for social justice, starting with Du Bois's work on the Philadelphia survey and the Chicago School of sociology under the leadership of Robert Park (Bogdan & Biklen, 2007). Because all this history swirls around committee relationships, having a good relationship with your advisor, particularly, and other committee members is important.

The committee's pedagogical purposes take shape as the dissertation is researched and written. The committee can provide advice and assistance, serve as a sounding board, offer support and critique, and articulate expectations during the process of producing the document. At the defense, the committee changes its role, somewhat, and becomes an examining committee. For both purposes, then, your committee is the audience for whom the document is written. This chapter addresses these concerns and discusses questions about committee formation, handling relationships with your committee, and working out conflicts—particularly choosing an advisor, working with a committee, power relations, (taking) criticism, conflicts and support, and negotiating differences. We begin with your committee as an audience for your work.

THE COMMITTEE AS AUDIENCE

Publishers and the people they hire to help them sell books think of books in terms of their markets. A market is the population at whom the book is aimed—the audience for whom authors write books or the people they imagine reading them. Markets might be juvenile readers, mystery fans, science-fiction devotees, or history buffs. If you want to develop your dissertation into a book, you might imagine your audience for the dissertation as those who would buy and read your book. But your audience for the dissertation is primarily your dissertation committee, and these committees have particular expectations of what a dissertation should look like. These expectations differ by university, but they are specific, and some common values reign.

It may sound insulting to compare a dissertation committee to a commercial market. Certainly the university does not usually demand that its students write in a style that would be commercially viable. But you always write for somebody. In this case, the "somebody" is not a jury of your peers. Your dissertation committee is made up of people with whom you (hopefully) have a personal relationship but who are also representatives of an academic institution or culture that is certifying you as capable of doctoral-level research. Although they are institutional representatives, they do not necessarily interpret their task similarly. Not only do various disciplines understand dissertations differently, but individual members of departments and disciplines also prefer different kinds of work. Some faculty may be attracted to dissertations written in an extremely personal style that reflects the auto-ethnographic approach exemplified in the work of Carolyn Ellis (1991, 1997, 2004), while others may be critical of this romanticizing of the self (Atkinson, Coffey, & Delamont, 2003). Critical race theorists emphasize the importance of centering the stories of marginalized people in a narrative mode (Duncan, 2002; Ladson-Billings, 2003; Solorzano & Yosso, 2002). Other faculty may encourage qualitative research in the mode of the Chicago School or the sort of institutional ethnography connected originally with the work of Dorothy Smith (1987, 2005). Some may promote theoretical dissertations informed by feminism or postcolonialism. Whatever their approach, they will want to see data. Because this is empirical work, they will want to see how you develop your analysis from your data and how your work fits in with the field you have designated it for.

You want to know something about your committee's specific expectations for your dissertation. There will be a buzz around your department about what specific faculty members' expectations are like, about what the process of working with a committee on a dissertation entails, and all of the backtalk that flows through university corridors. You can learn about expectations by talking to faculty members directly, but also by reading dissertations that are recommended to you as excellent. Since the dissertation advisor is particularly important, we start with this person and then move on to other committee members.

DISSERTATION ADVISORS

Your dissertation advisor is an important person in your life. You want to work with someone who is knowledgeable and experienced but who is also supportive. You want someone who will help you to write the best dissertation you are capable of doing but who will also understand the roadblocks you face. When you have scheduled a meeting with your advisor, for example, and the clinical depression you are experiencing keeps you from writing, you want an advisor who understands your situation. You want a sympathetic advisor when you send a memo like the following:

> Greetings.
>
> How are you?
>
> I'm overdue to check in and give you an update on my news. Unfortunately, the lapse is due to having been ill the last 4 months. I wasn't sure what the illness was until a few weeks ago, when I was finally diagnosed with Epstein-Barr virus, otherwise known as chronic fatigue. Since then, I have been consumed with pursuing various forms of treatments, all the while keeping my classes going.

It is the rare advisor who does not understand such a significant crisis. At the same time, you do not want an advisor who demands too little from you and who will let you schedule a defense when you are not ready and might be in danger of facing too many revisions or of not passing.

It is important to write a strong dissertation that has rich data, serious analysis, and makes a sound argument. You want to have a relationship with your advisor such that you can truthfully explain the complications you may face in the data or in your personal life. This means that you need to have a trusting relationship with your advisor; the best one is where you feel that your advisor is most concerned about your best interests. This situation is a little more complicated than it may appear at first glance. The advisor also has interests at stake in the relationship. If it is the advisor's first time chairing a committee, then he or she may feel pressure to perform well, to be as knowledgeable as possible, and to have a student who has "done well." If the advisor is invested in your performance, then when you write a good dissertation the advisor will glean some of the benefits. So, even when it works well, this relationship is a complicated one. It is for this reason that we underscore the importance of building trust in the relationship and of working to communicate well. We discuss these concerns more fully later in the chapter.

Choosing an Advisor

People—students and faculty—have many different styles of interacting and of working. This idea is nothing new, but it is something to think about when you choose an advisor and organize your dissertation committee. These styles can include formal, organized, casual, interactive, rule obeying, warm, and distant. When the students, advisors, and committee work together, they have to negotiate these styles in multiple combinations. Additionally, because professors hold more power than students, power relations always enter into the relationship—not always in straightforward ways, but always. Hopefully, when you ask a professor to chair your dissertation committee, you have already developed a relationship through working together on a project, having had the professor in several classes, or working with him or her as a teaching or research assistant. If you already have a relationship, then you know a little about the professor's style. Whatever you know about the faculty member before starting, you will learn more as the dissertation advances. One author, for example, has an informal style. Students sometimes think that informality signals an easy touch and are surprised when they find that her expectations are high.

We are writing as if you have numerous choices for a dissertation advisor. We have constructed this process as if there are multiple faculty you would like to have for a chair and all you must do is simply consider their different styles and choose the person with whom you feel most comfortable or who you think will help you to write the best dissertation. Of course, this is often not the case: There may only be two or three faculty in your department for you to choose between, or there may be only one person who knows something about your topic. Even if this is the case, the more knowledgeable you are about how relationships between dissertation advisors and their students work, the more influence you can have on how the process works.

Working with Your Advisor

You want your advisor to think that your project is interesting and important, and to expect you to do good work. If your advisor is new to the dissertation process, both of you will be learning simultaneously about working together. If your advisor has experience working with doctoral students, he or she will have expectations about how the process should go. The flexible advisor understands the process, has clear expectations and goals for you, and also is sensitive to your style of working, ways of thinking, and needs. When your advisor sees you as a person from whom he or she can learn, you will have a different relationship than if your efforts are seen as a way to promote the advisor's own work. You want your advisor to conceptualize the relationship between doctoral student and advisor as a kind of collaboration. The advisor has knowledge and particular understandings to offer, and you can increase your advisor's awareness of certain matters, ways of understanding problems, and new fields. You may also challenge your advisor in ways that are intellectually or politically interesting. In this kind of relationship, you may feel able to ask for help without worrying that doing so will make you look foolish. One student requested advice: "My problem is trying to summarize the arguments of the chapter without just repeating what I said in the chapter. Help!" She did not worry that she would appear unequal to the task.

We have said that you and your advisor know different things. Yet you are not equal to faculty members in the status hierarchy. This power differential is always important. Knowing different things sometimes leads to conflict with your advisor. Part of your task is to analyze the source of the conflict and try to verbally address it. Advisors bring to their relationships with students a long history of interaction with other students, so when they analyze each situation, they are placing it within this history. You, however, are advocating for your own work. One source of conflict, for example, may come from the differences in the literature you read. Not to stereotype, but the advisor might be familiar with the traditional literature in sociology, psychology, history of education, reading education, or social work, and the student might be interested in and familiar with more current or interdisciplinary work that addresses the topic in new ways (or the reverse can be true as well)

As advisors, we have frequently experienced situations with doctoral students where we have deeply admired the potential that the work promises and have insisted that the student rewrite chapters, add more data, or expand a conclusion. If you have a trusting relationship with your advisor, you may agree to the revisions even if, from your perspective, they do not seem necessary. Most frequently, in our experience, when the defense goes well, students will say something like, "My advisor insisted that I redo this, and at the time I was snarling under my breath, but now I'm so glad that I did." Producing a dissertation is a process of negotiation, just as doing fieldwork is a process of negotiating the focus with your informants. In this example, the advisor built on experience to insist on changes. If you feel that your advisor is too picky, you should discuss your perspectives and your interests. What you negotiate will probably lead to a better dissertation because you will have to articulate more clearly what you are doing, even if your advisor agrees that you have made good points.

WORKING WITH YOUR COMMITTEE

There are many issues to consider about the relationship between dissertation advisors and students, and the negotiations involved with a committee. Sometimes a fluid consensus establishes itself, where committee
members are collegial with one another and, because of shared interests
or values, flexibility, or other reasons, work together with little friction. All
the committee members may be excited by the candidate's work, believe
in the significance of the topic, and understand the theoretical orientation
that guides their colleagues' comments. Or they may share understandings
of changes that need to be made. The committee on a recent dissertation,
for example, agreed upon reading a near-to-final draft that the literature
review in the document was inadequate for the topic that the student was
addressing. The student hunkered down and expanded the review in significant ways to produce an award-winning dissertation. Sometimes, however, even though your committee members may be good scholars as
individuals and offer you insightful analysis and criticism about your work,
they offer you opposing ideas about revision. In one dissertation committee, one of the committee members wanted the student's work to be more
theoretical, while the other wanted it to be more descriptive. Here the role
of the chair was to negotiate between these friendly but opposing committee members. This kind of conflict occurred in a committee where all par-
ties were friendly, respectful, and flexible. The committee members did not
insist that their view was the only right way to understand the project.

Other times, this fluid consensus evaporates or was never there. Committee meetings can be tense; faculty members may not communicate well
with one another; fundamental disagreements about content, perspective,
or other issues may arise; or faculty may be working out conflicts they have
about other issues connected to work at these meetings. This is the night-
mare scenario you might dream about when you are feeling anxious about
the whole dissertation process. It rarely occurs at such a heightened level,
but it sometimes does happen. A faculty member can have much greater
expertise on a particular topic than other committee members and insist
that the student has "gotten it wrong." Committee members also can have
serious differences about what the data should look like, who the informants should be, what the analysis has to take into account, or how to theo-
rize about meaning.

One strategy to counteract conflictual interactions is to avoid leaving
communication with the committee until the end. While the dissertation
chair is the primary person with whom you interact, sending updates to
the whole committee, perhaps in the form of short memos about your
progress, is useful. If you do maintain regular contact with committee

members, they will not be surprised by your work when you are nearing the end of the process.

LEARNING LESSONS FROM FRUSTRATION

All doctoral students hit roadblocks. Sometimes these roadblocks come in the form of advisors and committee members. Doctoral students might find themselves thanking committee members one day and resenting them the next. This can last for the duration of a project. To prevent such frustrations from turning into battles with people who must approve your work and may provide recommendations and support later in your career, it is important to learn something that will help you even after you get a job: An open, calm demeanor and a willingness to accept and benefit from criticism can go a long way. What is important to remember is that in most circumstances committee members are trying to help you the best that they can given their experiences and perspectives on your work. Although you may disagree with their perspectives and not have had the experiences that they have had, other people may agree with them, including those who could end up considering you for a job or research grant.

One dissertation committee member urged a doctoral student conducting a nontraditional qualitative research project in education to develop a section of the dissertation that explained why the dissertation was important to education. The student felt that this was not necessary—that the connections were self-evident, and if they weren't, catch-phrases like "It's cultural studies" would explain them. With much resistance, the writer wrote the section. In the defense, the readers, who were not familiar with cultural studies theories, told him how much they appreciated his analysis of the relationship of his work to the field of education. Many months later, when the dissertation writer was interviewing for faculty positions, he realized how important it was to explain the significance of his dissertation topic to individuals not familiar with cultural studies and other nontraditional contexts of education. When he had been told to do this as a student, he felt like he would be selling out, talking down to his audience, and limiting the scope of his dissertation. Ultimately, he came to see that the advisor's experience and knowledge with academia, job searches, dissertation committees, and readers was a way of thinking that he did not have.

Another former doctoral student discussed how she, too, later learned to appreciate feedback from a committee member who, at the time, seemed only bent on frustrating her. As with many dissertation writers, the frustrations caused by questioning and critical committee members was only one blockade among others, including starting a new job, teaching three classes, supervising teachers, raising a family, and, ultimately, becoming sick partly because of the stress related to all this. But like other dissertation writers, she had support. And where the support did not help her, perseverance did. Ultimately, like the dissertation writer blending education and cultural studies, this student learned that, though difficult, the process of the committee member questioning and critiquing the theory section of her dissertation had given her valuable experience. She explained:

> I am not sure if my issues had more to do with the fact that I was a single working parent than that my dissertation was qualitative. The spring of my defense was really tough. I had started a new job in the fall and was teaching three classes in addition to supervising six new teachers, working toward an impending defense, and trying to be a good mom. It was quite literally making me sick. A couple things that kept me sane were my writing group, a supportive family, an understanding sponsor, and a deadline. The sticking point in my revisions was weaving in my theoretical framework. My sponsor and my second reader had slightly different conceptions of what constituted a theoretical framework for my study and how it helped to shape the study (social constructivist, or theories of teacher planning and inquiry-based learning). I had completed one draft in which the analysis was shaped by the literature on teacher planning and inquiry-based learning. My sponsor thought it was approaching completion. When my second reader read it, she was dismayed—and so was I! I had totally missed the mark according to her. In the meeting when she told me this, she asked which professor had I had for the qualitative research class. I reminded her that it was her. Yikes. That year I was teaching fourth grade full time at a new job, taking six points a term and parenting. After that meeting, the three of us met to discuss the shape of the dissertation. C and M [the two committee members] hashed out what my theoretical framework was and how that influenced the shape. At the same time, they both wanted me to have ownership. By that point, I didn't really care if I had ownership. They both had to agree that it was finished. I needed them to tell me what they were looking for. I felt (and still do) that the whole process is a bit of a game. (In my teaching, I would catch myself asking the students a leading question and waiting for them to guess the right answer. I find it very unfair when teachers do that and would always try to just tell the students what I was looking for. I needed my readers to acknowledge the fact that they were looking for something in particular and tell me what it was instead of my

trying to guess.) I came away from that meeting with an outline of how to reanalyze and reshape the data to tell the story through a sociocultural lens. I am lucky that I work pretty quickly. Given the guidance, I was able to revise my dissertation and defend that term. I even enjoyed revising because using the different framework allowed me to really get deeper into my original research question. Even though I got very frustrated with M's expectations, in the end I was really glad she was my second reader because of the insights she helped me gain into the process of research, the theory I was using, and the data I had collected. The funny part of the story is that at my defense, one of the other committee members asked why I used such fancy theoretical language all over the place. M answered for me, saying that she "made me do it." I told her later that I could have answered that question easily—because of the insights that using such "fancy" theoretical language helped me gain in my understanding of the events unfolding in the classroom in which I conducted my research.

In both of the examples just described, the revisions turned out to be worthwhile. And while it is indeed true that you will want recommendations for positions after the defense, it is important to examine the source of any disagreement you have with your committee so that you are not just accepting their suggestions because they are faculty and you are a student. Again, if you have a relationship with your advisor in which respect and trust are mutual, your advisor should listen to your views and be influenced by them. Where the differences between you concern how extensive your literature review should be or whether you should discuss an abusive interaction you had with an informant in the methodology chapter, the differences may be straightforward. When you are discussing your different views about your work, you are discussing your work.

In other cases, however, differences based on generation, gender, class conflicts, or racial politics can engender conflicts that direct discussion about the issues may not be able to resolve since the differences are about more than the thing itself. Work from feminist, critical theoretical, or antiracist locations may spur you to want to challenge the traditions for writing a dissertation. You may want to use a more personal narrative, alternative ethnographic approaches, or a strong political argument. If these are the differences you have with your advisor, you must talk about these differences, not the issue that has seemed to set off the conflict. Of course, faculty may also challenge you to address concerns about race, class, gender, or disability that you did not think were central to your topic. It is important not to stereotype the perspectives of either faculty or students.

THINKING ABOUT CRITICISM

One of the most important parts of your relationship with your dissertation committee is the criticism you get from them. We are not talking about mean-spirited, writing-you-off criticism, which students rarely hear from faculty but which is often the form you imagine criticism takes. We define criticism, rather, as useful commentary that recognizes the potential of your work and offers you some vision of how to reach this potential. Perhaps *criticism* is not even the right word; maybe we should call it *analysis* or *critique* of your work. Since it is commonly referred to as *criticism*, however, we will use that term.

You want good criticism of your drafts, your ideas, your data, and your analysis because it demonstrates engagement with your work, your ideas, and yourself as an agent in the world. It means that your committee takes you seriously and offers you readings of your work from their vantage points. The criticism that committee members give you is not always "right," or at least not always "right on target." But even when committee members give you criticism that you think is not right, it can show you that you have not written for the audience that you must reach in a way that they can understand. You can use this kind of criticism to revise the section or sections that the committee members critiqued.

The criticism that committee members offer may sometimes make you feel joyous because you see that the committee members understand what you were trying to accomplish and the changes that are suggested make sense. You might think of criticism as another set of eyes on your material, representing a point of view that is not as bound up in the text as you are but that cares about the text and is invested in your work. Good criticism not only tells you what is not working for the reader but also gives you a direction, or some choices about direction, that you can take. A good outcome is for you to leave the committee member's office saying to yourself, "That makes sense."

It is more difficult to feel good about criticism if you are pushing to finish the document by a deadline that is too close. You must expect to do drafts of your writing, and you cannot expect too much sympathy from committee members who are unwilling to make too many compromises about their expectations for your work. New faculty members often feel pressured to accept student comments that they have to finish by such and such a date because of visa problems, a new job, forthcoming childbirth, or an impending marriage. These events should not dictate, even though they can influence, the quality of your dissertation. On the other hand, the dissertation is only one research project, not the only one.

If you can view criticism as taking your work seriously, you may be able to look more positively on communication in this vein. Criticism does not necessarily mean that committee members do not "like" your work, just as lack of criticism does not necessarily mean that the committee values your work. "Liking" and "not liking" are too superficial to have much meaning in relation to your project.

The role of the dissertation advisor in relation to criticism changes over the course of the project. While you are preparing the dissertation, the role of the advisor is to push you to write a high-quality work. The good advisor should offer criticism (and encouragement) and is not fulfilling the role if this does not happen. At the defense, however, the advisor shifts tasks and works to decrease the number of revisions you have to do. The advisor cannot protect you from revisions, but he or she does act as an advocate for your work.

THINKING ABOUT COMMITTEES

The dissertation has many purposes. It is a capstone to a rigorous graduate school education. It is also a stepping-stone to a job, in which (in the case of academic jobs) one may be expected to make a presentation on the dissertation, to develop a research agenda based on it, and possibly to teach classes related to it. The dissertation must also represent your abilities to develop theory, to integrate literature, to conduct research, and to write like a scholar. Dissertation committee members often have different concerns and areas of interest, in fact, the best committees may be comprised of those who ask different tasks from the same student: One committee member might want you to develop the theory part of the dissertation (to use the "fancy language"), partly because it is important to know theory and partly because it is important to be able to refer to theories in a job interview. Another might want a more developed research method section. Yet another might ask for greater focus on a topic that other members may want culled from the dissertation. Learning to be flexible, to synthesize and find a common ground among critiques, and to be patient and persistent pays off for the dissertation—and also prepares you for the publishing world. (Who says that three reviewers will all agree when they evaluate your manuscript?) It also prepares you for promotion and tenure committees that also may not agree on the work that you do.

Feedback on your dissertation rarely comes in neat packages, and this can cause frustrations. But learning to make sense of and work within the context of disparate viewpoints often improves a dissertation. Learning this during the writing of your dissertation is better than learning it later during the crucial first few years of your job—or never at all. This is not to say that you should be thankful for the frustration and the maneuvering you may feel yourself doing endlessly, but the purposes of dissertations, as noted earlier, are numerous. Those who force themselves to benefit from the process have added to the purposes just discussed the knowledge and skills to act professionally, persistently, and with understanding and confidence.

CHAPTER 4

The Protection of Human Subjects

The protection of human subjects is an ethical question for social scientists. Research projects can raise many ethical concerns. When Burton Blatt and colleagues founded the Center on Human Policy at Syracuse University, the Center's research staff traveled to various institutions for people with intellectual disabilities to investigate the abuse of human beings at these places. They faced ethical dilemmas because they did not know what to do when they came up against scenes that raised moral questions for them. If they saw an inmate chained to a wall, what was the ethical response? Should they immediately tell the world what was happening in these institutions to create immediate change? Should they yell and scream to get the attention of the administrators in the hope that such attention would jumpstart better treatment? Should they continue to collect data at institutions around the Northeast to document for a journal article how widespread the inhumane treatment of human beings was? They faced an ethical dilemma that was not easy to resolve with a set of rules or procedures. They needed intense discussions with a variety of people to come to their decisions about how to act.

This chapter does not address this important ethical dilemma, though these kinds of discussions are vital. Rather, it is much more practically focused on the kinds of ethical questions that Institutional Review Boards (IRBs) address through their monitoring systems. Every university requires those doing research with human subjects—with a few exceptions, such as historians conducting oral histories with public figures—to apply for and receive approval to conduct their research. This chapter addresses some of the more general ways of thinking about how IRBs perceive and construct the protection of human subjects, some bits of advice about how to apply for and receive IRB approval, and a few stories of problems some applicants have faced. To find out the specific requirements of your university, you must look on its website, where every university posts its forms and requirements. Since many qualitative methods classes and texts also address IRB approval, you may find more information there. Our experience as qualitative researchers and our many years of service on an IRB have both contributed to our discussion of the protection of human subjects.

THE FUNCTIONS OF AN IRB

IRBs were created to regulate research conducted by university faculty, students, and staff in order to both ensure as nearly as possible that the research is conducted in an ethical manner and to protect the university as much as possible from the risk of endangering research subjects. When you feel frustrated with the paperwork, it is important to remember that these boards are as much about risk management as about ethics. Oversight committees define research as scholarship involving human subjects with the purpose of producing generalizable knowledge.

The impetus for IRBs stems from the history of ethical failures in research. The IRB is a response primarily to medical research that took advantage of informants and harmed them. It has its origins in the Nuremberg trials, where the experimentation on and mistreatment of prisoners by doctors in Nazi concentration camps raised questions about how to set guidelines for ethical behavior toward patients. Another important and famous case that contributed to the founding of institutional review boards also involved medical research. The government-run Tuskegee experiment involved poor Black sharecroppers in Tuskegee, Alabama, who were in the last stages of syphilis. Between 1932 and 1972, around 600 African American men in Alabama became guinea pigs for American medical research (Reverby, 2000). Because these were people without power, the government felt it could experiment on them without incrimination. So these men were not informed of the nature of their illness and were left to die without treatment. They were told that they had "bad blood" (hence the title of the well-known book about this experiment [Jones, 1993]). The medical researchers wanted to see how the disease ravaged the bodies of the men, so they waited for the men to die so that they could do autopsies. These are the kinds of cases that animated the founding of IRBs, which represent an institutional response to a concern about how one handles ethical problems in conducting research.

IRBs take shape in different ways. At some universities, particularly those with medical schools, there are multiple IRBs to handle different kinds of research. At the University of Wisconsin there is an IRB devoted solely to educational research. Other universities have two IRBs, one for social science research and one for medical and "hard" scientific research, while many have single IRBs that handle all of the proposals submitted. In this latter case, having representation from disciplines that the different proposals come from is especially important. Again, the variety in IRBs means that you need to learn what your university's procedures and practices are.

The IRB cares about many issues involving the protection of human subjects. One of the most significant is that researchers design their studies so that their informants can refuse to participate. IRBs want to make sure that subjects do not feel coerced into participation. You want your informants to agree to participate in your study knowing what the demands will be on them. How much time will their participation take? How will you protect their confidentiality? Are there any occasions when you will not be able to protect their confidentiality? Will the benefits of the research outweigh the risks to the informants? These are the kinds of questions IRB members bring to proposals they read.

The question of benefits and risks means that when IRBs consider your proposal, they take into account how you have designed your study. While the task of board members is not to approve or disapprove of your particular research design or judge your sophistication as a researcher, they do need to make sure that there will be some benefit to the research. Therefore, if you have proposed a design that board members find has huge problems, you may get comments back with an "approval withheld" notice addressing your discussion of methods.

NAVIGATING THE POLICIES OF IRBS

IRBs around the country are moving toward greater regulation and inflexibility. The biomedical research paradigm applies to both social science and medical research. Hence, with the deaths in recent years of patients/research subjects at the University of Pennsylvania and at Johns Hopkins University, IRBs have cracked down on all research with greater bureaucracy. Social science research, which involves much less risk to subjects, still faces this increased bureaucracy. Even with the increased regulation, however, IRBs at different universities differ from one another. Some are more flexible with social science research while some are not. Some take a punitive approach, while others do not.

Policies of IRBs differ depending on how the IRB chair, board members, and regulatory compliance administrators interpret federal guidelines. At Syracuse University, for example, research that students conduct under course supervision is allowed to proceed without IRB approval, but at other institutions this approach is forbidden. At some universities, students can use data collected without IRB approval for a course assignment in their dissertations along with other, IRB-approved data. At others, they may not. These differences are the result of different approaches to the guidelines. The IRB permits data collected for one purpose to be used for another, so according to the federal regulations, this is permissible. If the primary purpose of collecting data in a methods class is to learn the skills of qualitative methods, then the data can be used for a second purpose, such as supporting the dissertation, once the first purpose is no longer primary. Your university may not, however, interpret the regulations this way, and though you may protest, you may not succeed in getting the board to acquiesce.

Oral consent is getting much more difficult to count as consent for any kind of qualitative research including participant observation and in-depth interviewing. IRBs tend to have little understanding of cultural contexts that differ from what quantitative academic culture understands. In international or subcultural research fieldwork, for example, certain communities may be offended by having to sign a form, as people do not typically interact with each other in that way. When oral consent is necessary for the safety of the informants, however, you might be able to make an argument that the IRB will understand. In this case, oral consent would mean that no written document could link the informant's name to the project. If you were studying refugees or detainees, for example, you would need to have this protection for your subjects.

Procedures for qualitative research are so different from those for medical and statistical research that many IRBs struggle with how to respond to proposals from ethnographers (see Hemmings, 2006). Many IRBs, for instance, do not understand participant observation. For example, if the researcher is following around a child that a classroom teacher is trying to include, how do you think about the question of permission? The researcher should have to get the child's and the family's permission, but such permission should not be needed from everyone in the class, as some boards may require. The general guideline should be "don't deceive."

There is a widespread position among IRBs that there should be no covert research. The understanding is that IRB rules require all research to be overt and above board. But actually, according to the rules, this is not true. The rules say that each application for covert research should be scrutinized. To the extent appropriate, researchers should debrief and tell people afterward (Taylor, 2006). Rebekah Nathan (the pseudonym used by the professor at an Arizona university who pretended to be a college student in order to study student life) lived in a college dorm for two semesters and attended classes, all undercover, and had her research approved by her university's IRB (Nathan, 2005b). She described the numerous ethical issues that she faced even after she received IRB approval, issues that were directly related to her use of covert research. One concerned using talk that she overheard as data:

> I also overheard many dialogues through the thin walls of my dorm room. Almost every night I went to sleep to chatter and laughter from the adjacent rooms and was privy to informative waves of gossip and drama. While I learned plenty from such conversations, it was clear to me that I should not take notes or otherwise record what I heard.
>
> But what about public conversations in the halls, in my classes, and in my study groups when the information was shared with me on the assumption that I was a student, and only a student? The questions regarding my data seemed to grow more numerous as time went on. I realized that my level of comfort and certainty was shifting with the depth and quality of my relationships and with seeing the data in their human context—as incidents, stories, and conversations attached to real people. When the writing process began, push came to shove, and choices had to be made.
>
> As I wrote, I tried to keep in mind the students with whom I'd gone to college. Would I be comfortable saying what I was writing that moment, in that chapter, if I were saying it to them? I tried projecting, too: Would I be comfortable if I were a student and recognized in a book, written by a professor at my own university, an informal conversation that I thought I was having privately with a classmate? Those considerations radically changed how I wrote, and new "rules" of a sort emerged. (Nathan, 2005a)

Nathan was unmasked by an investigative journalist who suggested that she gave too many details about the pseudonymous university she described, but even so, she had received permission to do a study using covert qualitative methods. (For another view on covert qualitative research see Herrera, 1999.)

IRBs depend on voluntary compliance. This is central to all IRB policies because coercion runs counter to the approach. If the university does not foster an atmosphere of confidence in researchers, people will try to get around the IRB and the board will be unable to promote either ethical research or the values needed to uphold it.

STANDARD FORMS FOR AN IRB REVIEW

Each university has a standard template for consent forms, so part of learning to do research at a university involves learning the vocabulary of the IRB. This includes knowing the differences between full board review, exempt research, and expedited review. Studies where nobody can be harmed are considered exempt research. For example, a doctoral student recently applied for expedited review (where there is little risk and the proposal does not have to be considered for full board review) to study the perspectives of bilingual teachers at an urban elementary school. The project involved interviewing all the teachers in bilingual classrooms, a former bilingual teacher, and the principal. The student received her form back saying that her research was approved as an exempt study and did not have to be considered by the board again for 5 years. She had not realized how little risk was involved in the project, but the chair of the board understood this.

But, of course, qualitative studies can involve risk. Most boards are particularly conscious of any kind of investigation involving sex—including studies of sex education, date rape, counseling on sexual problems, or domestic abuse. Any student doing work on such topics will have to come before full board review.

The IRB requires that all researchers applying for IRB approval state the risk involved in their research. Most forms specifically say that all research involves risk. We have a list of risks that we can routinely use in IRB applications and that we advise our students are useful to name if they cannot think of the risks involved. Your questions in an interview, for example, might make informants uneasy when they recall parts of their lives that involved struggle. The purpose of this question on IRB forms is to stimulate researchers to consider hidden forms of risk in their projects that they might not have noticed. However, sometimes the only risk is that you are wasting someone's time. Do you make up a risk? Unfortunately, IRBs promote this kind of thinking.

The templates used on IRB forms demand that you address required elements and particular issues in specific ways. The country seems to be moving toward a single template for all research (Taylor, 2006). These forms are foreign to social science research, especially to qualitative approaches. When bureaucracy increases in IRBs, as is currently happening, authority moves from the faculty on the IRB to the administrative staff, and this shift constricts discretionary judgment. This increasingly bureaucratic approach fosters ritualistic and bureaucratic forms of compliance.

A major issue for those of us who use qualitative methods is how IRBs understand qualitative research. If IRB members know very little about the approach, they will always compare applications for approval from qualitative researchers to the standard they hold for quantitative researchers. For example, they will not understand the idea of emergent design—how knowing all your questions in advance can signal a weak rather than a strong design, and so forth. Many IRBs do not think that qualitative research is "real" research and judge proposals to be "fishing expeditions."

Oral histories, as they have been traditionally practiced in history departments, do not fall under the purview of the IRB. Historians generally use oral history with public figures, interviewing, for example, political and military leaders. This sort of oral history is different from how sociologists use the term to mean interviewing ordinary people about everyday life.

SPECIFIC ADVICE

Exempt research. Ask whether your study can qualify for an exemption. Some IRBs will not grant them, but the investigation is worth the effort. Syracuse University's policy is to provide approval to exempt research for five years, but each university can set its own policy. The label of exempt research applies to a range of qualitative studies, such as public observation, interviews, and open-ended surveys. The federal government has developed six categories of exempt research, some of which apply to qualitative projects. If your study takes place in an educational setting and involves the use of regular pedagogy—that is, teaching that would be done anyway whether or not you were participating in the pedagogy or reviewing it—it qualifies as exempt. If you are conducting research on public officials, it is exempt. If you are using data that are recorded in a manner such that people cannot be identified, then your research is exempt—for example, if you are looking at anonymous students, without identifiers, commenting on their grade point averages. While this example might seem foreign to the qualitative researcher (since qualitative data only have meaning in some context), it might be possible for a qualitative researcher to use data already collected for a big project where the researcher did not know the names of the particular settings, or perhaps even the state where the data were collected.

Methodological soundness. The qualitative researcher needs to be prepared to lay out the established qualitative tradition in his or her application. Especially for IRBs with little experience with this approach, you will need to document how this research tradition works. References to the qualitative literature should be provided.

Participant observation. In the methods section of the IRB application, you need to say how you will identify yourself in settings where you will be doing participant observation. You do not have to take a consent form out of your bag when you are observing them, but when you start questioning people in a participant observation session (for example, if you and your informants are eating in a restaurant and you want to ask them about what you have just observed), you need to say who you are.

Informed consent. A significant concern for IRBs and for everyone doing research is the issue of consent. For researchers doing participant observation, the question is particularly tricky because each person you observe is not equally placed as an informant, and you need to make decisions about the appropriate time to say that you are a researcher and ask the person you are observing to sign the consent form. Because of the feeling of contingency that exists while doing participant observation, you may not always be able to follow the template exactly, even though you need to address it in your application form. The website of Syracuse University, the federal IRB website, and perhaps the website at your own university, explain where waivers to written consent are possible, along with the elements of consent.

BALANCING ETHICS AND STRATEGY

When you want to study some but not all people in a setting, there are ways of writing the application that help you be attentive to ethics but make it less necessary to get permission from others in the setting you may not be interested in studying. Such situations might include studying some, but not all, nursing students in a lab setting; female, but not male, workers at a fast-food restaurant; or students with learning disabilities in a certain class. You should be careful in your application about the level of detail you share regarding other people who may also spend time in the setting if you do not want to be forced to get everyone's permission. Don't describe others so that they can be identified. This approach is both ethical and circumspect.

IRBs have incredible power, visible in the fact that no administrative appeal exists if the application to the IRB is rejected. This means that there is no recourse for you if the IRB rejects your project. The university administration can disapprove what the IRB approves, but not the opposite. There is no appeal, though you may be able to ask for reconsideration depending on the particular IRB. In addition to rejection, the three responses you can get are approval, which means your research is approved with no changes needed; provisional approval, which means that you need to make certain (minor) changes in order to receive approval; and withheld approval, which means that your application has serious problems that must be addressed and reconsidered by the whole board.

The IRB is not just about ethics in research, however. It is also about risk to the university and compliance with federal regulations regarding university research. The Syracuse University *IRB Handbook*, for example, says that the IRB always has to balance its "educational" and "regulatory" roles. The *Handbook* states that the best context for conducting ethical research occurs in settings where the researchers' "internalized" values, rather than a set of procedures regarding moral behavior, guide the research process so that the educational function works to create the internalized values while the regulatory function works to make sure that human subjects are protected.

A RESEARCHER'S STORY: GETTING IRB APPROVAL

For a qualitative study of violence in a city school, one researcher attempted to get IRB approval to conduct research on school social work. The plan was to shadow a social worker during one schoolyear. Shadowing a school social worker involved attending meetings (such as Pupil Placement Team [PPT] meetings), sitting in on consultations with students, and interviewing the social worker several times during the year. When the researcher submitted his application to the IRB committee, it was denied. In the rejection letter, the chair of the IRB stated that "the committee was concerned that several issues surrounding the protection of human subjects were not clear" and specified three areas where clarity was needed. To the researcher, the concerns of the IRB seemed legitimate. They wanted more clarity regarding how informed consent would be obtained from the social worker; they had concerns about who would have access to the data; and they wanted to know what adults besides the social worker might be interviewed, since the researcher had mentioned that informal interviews might be conducted with other social workers in other schools to test the generalizability of the data collected in the one school. In the rejection letter, the researcher was invited to attend the next IRB meeting to discuss the application and clarify these points. Though a minor inconvenience, the researcher was more than willing to attend the next meeting in order to resolve the issue.

At the next meeting, the committee asked the researcher to explain, "in your own words," what the research project entailed. When the researcher mentioned that he would be conducting interviews, one committee member remarked that he had not submitted the interview questionnaire. The researcher responded that there was no questionnaire because the interviews would be conducted informally. The same committee member wanted to know "how can you conduct an interview without a questionnaire?" The researcher said that he could submit a set of questions that were likely to be asked at an interview. This seemed to suffice, especially after another committee member, more familiar with semistructured and informal interviews, defended the researchers' decision to not have a questionnaire. The committee chair (who was the same person to defend the researcher) then proceeded to address each of the three issues that needed more clarity. The researcher clarified each of the issues, and the chair asked him to submit the clarifications and interview questions before the next IRB meeting. It seemed that the issue was resolved. But then the member who had raised the issue about the questionnaire remarked, as if seeing the point for the first time: "It says here in your application that you will be attending meetings that the social worker attends. What meetings might this include?" The researcher pointed out that he had listed the possible meetings he would attend and showed the committee where the list was in the application. The same committee member suddenly let out a little gasp after seeing the list. She said, "It says here you will be attending PPT meetings." The researcher said he might, since much of the social worker's day was taken up with these meetings. The committee member then told the rest of the committee that she could not accept the application if it involved a "third party attending PPTs." The researcher echoed the concern raised by the committee member, remarking that PPT meetings involved delicate issues, dealt with special education placements, and usually included parents and "protected subjects," including minors with disabilities. The researcher also remarked that he would not be a "third party" but that, in fact, many people attended these meetings. In addition to social workers, PPT meetings also included parents, school psychologists, administrators, special education teachers, school counselors, and sometimes interns and student teachers. The researcher told the committee, "I can understand the concerns you have raised in your letter to me, but this is a new concern. I'd be happy to address it in my clarification letter." The committee member shot back, "This is not something you can just clarify. This is about the law. Do you know that this is federal law, the protection of subjects."

The researcher emphasized once again that he was aware of the gravity of the research and the protection that needed to be ensured. He reiterated that he understood the concerns raised by the committee member but also felt that it was possible to conduct such research without violating protection laws. Two other committee members agreed that something could be worked out and asked the researcher to clarify what the observations of PPT meetings would entail. The meeting was adjourned shortly after this.

During the week, a member of the IRB approached the researcher and told him that one member of the committee had a "personal stake" in the fact that the researcher would be attending PPT meetings. She did not mention the IRB member by name, but, to the researcher, it was clear whom she was talking about. Without saying so, she also intimated that the IRB member had a child in special education and had, as a parent, attended PPT meetings; and it was clear that this has been a very stressful experience for her. The researcher had a better understanding of why the IRB member was reacting as she was. He wasn't sure if the IRB member's child went to the school where he would be conducting his research, but he doubted it.

At the next meeting, the IRB member was less hostile, and it seemed to the researcher either that she had decided not to be as challenging as the last time or that someone had spoken to her, since it was clear that at least two of the other members of the IRB, including the chair, were not pleased that she had been so challenging. The researcher submitted a letter clarifying the three points that had initially needed clarification and a separate letter clarifying the issue of PPT meetings. In the letter, he reiterated the delicacy of the research, acknowledged the importance of informed consent and the "protection of human subjects," and detailed how he would ask for informed consent and protect those who participated in PPT meetings. Before each of the PPT meetings, he would introduce himself to the group, state his reason for attending the meeting, and ask if anyone there would rather he not attend the meeting. If all agreed that he could stay, he would; if anybody wished him to leave, he would leave. This seemed to suffice. The IRB member who had protested earlier remained rather quiet and read the two letters from the researcher carefully. All agreed that the researcher had provided enough information for them to make a decision. The chair told the researcher that he should expect a letter informing him of their decision. The chair was pleasant and seemed to suggest by his demeanor that the group would accept the IRB request. Before adjourning, the member who had protested earlier said to the researcher, "I hope you have learned something from this experience." The researcher said that he had.

What could a researcher learn from this experience? In a nutshell, there are several lessons to be learned, including that it is important to work with IRB committee members on their own terms and to be patient. Even when you feel that they are making a poor decision, or do not understand your research, you must be persistent without being "off-putting." You need to understand that the decisions IRB committees come to about your research are not necessarily decisions about your particular research. Decisions are sometimes made for reasons that are political and personal.

IRBs differ from each other. Some are punitive; others are not. Some have members who understand qualitative methods; others do not. Some have more discretion than others to interpret federal guidelines. One of the implications of this for those of you who plan to become faculty members is not to assume that the new IRB is the same as the one where you got your degree.

CHAPTER 5

The Qualitative Proposal

What is the proposal's relationship to the dissertation? The structure of the dissertation proposal in most programs is organized around what works best for the quantitative proposal—that is, that you prepare the proposal before doing the research. Qualitative proposals, on the other hand, should actually be written after you have already collected some of the data so that you know what the dissertation will focus on. Ideally, you should collect between one-quarter and one-third of your data before you write the proposal, though many factors can complicate an individual situation. When you first start doing your research, you need to cast the net so widely that you will find it difficult to write a proposal on the topic because you do not quite know what the topic is. After some time in the field, though, you do know what you will be working on and will be able to write a meaningful proposal. The proposal is important to the research because it serves as an agreement between you and your committee about what you will be working on, it helps you get started, and it facilitates the structure of the dissertation. A proposal forces you to chart a direction, to limit the scope of the project, and to gain clarity about what you are investigating.

Your department or university may have specific requirements about the length of the proposal. Some universities have a 30-page limit, specifying a 12-point font and double-spacing, without the references or footnotes. Others specify that the dissertation proposal be essentially the first three chapters of the dissertation, which are the introduction, the literature review, and the methods and procedures chapter. This requirement is more difficult for the qualitative than the quantitative researcher for a number of reasons. First, you don't do your complete literature review before you collect the data because of the inductive slant of the qualitative approach. Your fieldwork and data analysis guide you to specific literatures or theoretical works that you need to consult. Second, the methods chapters of qualitative researchers must discuss their fieldwork experiences, so this chapter cannot be completely written until after you have completed fieldwork. If your department has specific requirements, you obviously need to be attentive to these. From our perspective, 20 pages is an adequate length for a dissertation proposal. Certainly, 30 pages should be the outside limit for the qualitative proposal. Two aspects of qualitative research—the uncertain outcome of the qualitative project, and the process of first casting the net widely and then narrowing down the focus of your project—mean that the proposal is only a guide to what you will do, not a detailed account of what will actually happen. It is an important guide, but it is not like a contract. In some fields, for example, writing the proposal means that you have written the bulk of the dissertation, but this is not the case for the qualitative researcher.

In this chapter we first discuss what should be in a proposal and the order the sections should follow. Again, you should follow any specific guidelines that your university has for the proposal if they differ from these suggestions. Then we address some common questions that arise about the proposal itself.

STATEMENT OF THE PROBLEM
AND PURPOSE OF THE STUDY

The introduction states the problem and the purpose of your study. You can write an introduction that addresses both sections without specifically naming them as such, or you can separate them out with their own headings. The statement of the problem addresses the question: What is the issue? As the introductory section of your proposal, the statement of the problem describes the big issue that you want to address. Later on in this section, we will take three examples of big issues that students were interested in exploring for their dissertations and contrast them with the smaller piece of that issue that they investigated in the dissertation itself. We refer to this smaller piece of the issue as the purpose of the study, which we discuss in the next section of this chapter. Again, the problem of the study is at one level of abstraction, and your study addresses this problem through a particular entry point. If the problem you are interested in is, say, racism in higher education, domestic violence, the teaching of reading, or the ways students and professors communicate with each other, you have to figure out which piece of these huge topics you will address. These pieces become the purpose of your study.

It may sound like the purpose of the study section is more important than the statement of the problem because the purpose of the study specifically describes what your project takes up, but the statement of the problem actually sets the larger picture and provides a framework that anchors your work. It connects it to a particular way of seeing the purpose in context. A study of educational travel that is framed in the context of power relations differs from one that is concerned about expanding the horizons of college students, or one that addresses informal education over the lifespan, or one that is interested in specific social groups as markets for educational travel. And studies of female elementary school teachers will differ depending on whether the interests of the researcher center on student achievement, social reproduction, or discourses of gender. So the statement of the problem is significant because it tells the reader how to think about the purpose of your study.

Though we have just said that the statement of the problem comes first in the proposal, it is not actually completely separate from the purpose of the study. Dissertation proposal writing is not linear in the sense that sections are definitively separate from one another and always follow one another in order. These two sections should be somewhat woven together because the reader needs to know what you will be working on in order to read thoughtfully about your take on the larger issue. As a rule of thumb, you should always have at least one sentence that states the purpose of your study on the first page of your proposal, preferably in the first paragraph, even though you will need to repeat this sentence in a slightly different form later on. As readers, for example, we may wonder why the author is talking about the teaching of reading in a particular way unless we know that the work will be about the role of reading specialists in elementary schools. Here is an example from Kathleen Farrell's dissertation proposal "Backstage Politics: Media Activism and Social Change on TV." She ends the first paragraph of the proposal with a statement about her dissertation topic:

> Currently, NBC's Emmy Award winning sitcom, *Will and Grace*, is one of the most popular prime time series, frequently capturing top ratings in Nielsen's weekly lists, often winning its timeslot and stealing large audience shares. It has two gay characters in lead roles. On cable, Showtime's number one series, *Queer as Folk*, known for its numerous and often explicit gay sex scenes, "didn't cause World War III," according to executive producer Tony Jonas, leading Showtime to introduce a second show, *The L Word*, which also focuses on the lives of nonheterosexual characters. Yet, it was only [in] 1997 that Ellen DeGeneres, of ABC's *Ellen*, had to fight with Disney executives for permission to "come out," through her fictional character, on TV. This significant shift in queer television characters and storylines suggests that there have been various forces working behind the scenes to influence this transformation of TV content. Therefore, this dissertation project will investigate the advocates who work to bring televised visibility to queer people through their activist efforts with the entertainment TV industry by examining their

labors as well as the perspectives they hold on this kind of work. (Unpublished dissertation proposal, 2004)

Even though she continues her discussion of the problem (the representation of LGBTQ [lesbian, gay, bisexual, transgendered, and questioning] people on television), she has communicated to readers early on in the proposal about what they should hold in their minds while they are reading about the larger issue of how television programming represents a particular population. Next, we look at three examples of the big issues that former doctoral students took up that grounded their specific projects.

Three Examples

Whenever you make decisions about what aspect of the problem you will attempt to study, there are usually both practical and methodological reasons that prompt your choice. When you explain your decisions, however, you need to offer solid, methodologically defensible reasons for your actions, as "convenience samples" are not a strong defense. When you have funding that enables you to have a national sample or do a longitudinal study, you should always describe how the funding enabled you to undertake the work. Additionally, you can imagine that the students whose work we discuss might not describe the process in the same way we do. Our social locations differ, and so do our perspectives.

Example 1. Jeff Mangram wanted to do a dissertation on schools and popular culture. As a former social studies teacher, he was interested in how popular culture became a space in high school where students could bring in their knowledge about the world and where teachers had to confront their authority—epistemological and pedagogical—in relation to this space. This was the general issue that Jeff was interested in, but he had a series of decisions to make about how to narrow his study. Would he investigate this issue from the perspective of students who continually challenged the acceptable limits of what popular culture was allowed in schools? Should he do a case study of a single high school where he could explore the perspectives of students, teachers, administrators, and even parents about popular culture practices? As he thought through his choices, he developed criteria that would influence his decision. Since his field is social studies education, he decided that he should narrow his focus to the field of social studies so that he could contribute to a needed literature in this field. He decided that he would interview and do participant observation in social studies teachers' classrooms, focusing entirely on the teachers' perspectives. He gave up the views of young people themselves, because he decided that he wanted to see how the teachers understood what young people were about in relation to their popular culture. A few interviews that he did before writing his proposal suggested that many teachers took what Jeff called a "protectionist" approach to students, identifying their role as a barrier between the students and a dangerous world out there. Finally, because he wanted to have a diverse sample and because so many of the social studies teachers in the city and surrounding communities where he would do his study were white, Jeff decided to expand the geographic location of interviews and observations in order to gather a racially and ethnically diverse sample of social studies teachers. In the end, the purpose of his study was to examine "how social studies teachers make meaning of media and popular culture and how they negotiate these meanings or perspectives in their personal lives and in their pedagogical approaches in the classroom" (Mangram, 2006).

Example 2. From the time she entered her doctoral program, Kristen Luschen knew that she wanted to do a dissertation on sex and adolescents. She was interested in policy related to how schools handle different concerns related to teenagers and sex—concerns such as sex education, the different contexts that the levels of racial and class diversity in a school create, teen pregnancy, school-based health clinics, gender issues in relation to sex, and sexual identity. This is a topic that school officials are nervous about "outsiders" studying because, for example, parents have such widely divergent views about it. Through some groundwork, she heard about a couple of women who were trying to expand contraceptive services to a greater number of students in an urban district. One of these women was an administrator who recognized a problem in the district, and the other was also an administrator who, through the organizing efforts of the other administrator, was brought on board. Kristen developed a rapport with these players and got permission to shadow them while they pursued their goal. However, the district set up roadblocks almost immediately. While Kristen had gained permission to interview the administrators, go to meetings with them, and hang out while they strategized, there were actually very few of these occasions in which to participate. Kristen realized that she could use the data she had from the interviews as part of a study, but they were inadequate for a dissertation. She decided that she would reframe the dissertation to look at how adults in different locations in a single school district worked to help empower girls around their sexual lives, and what happened. One case concerned the administrators described above who were trying to expand contraceptive services. She also found two other cases to investigate: child-care educators in a day-care center for high school mothers located at a high school and a teacher in a sex education class for pregnant or parenting teens. So the purpose of her study, *Empowering Prevention? Adolescent Female Sexuality, Advocacy, and Schooling* (Luschen, 2005), was to describe and analyze the perspectives on sex education for young women of adult educators who worked in different capacities in schools in a single district. The dissertation argued that in spite of these adults' strong commitment to empowering young women through information and commitment to their getting an education, the current climate of abstention and the prevailing social discourses that see girls as needing protection created tremendous barriers. These educators' good intentions were not strong enough to overcome social constraints.

Example 3. Cerri Banks knew that she wanted to study Black women in higher education. She wanted "intersectionality"—the different identities that people hold around their racial, gendered, sexual, and class-based subjectivities—to frame her study because she believed that when people are lumped together under a single label, their individual stories are rendered invisible. She wanted to look at how individual Black female students navigated their educational careers at the university even though they faced racism and gender discrimination. Originally, she thought she might undertake a case study of African American women students at a predominantly white university, but then she received an opportunity to work on a national grant that was studying university campuses around the country that were quite different from one another. The extremely varying cultures at these different institutions enabled her to explore the narratives of African American female students who came from very different communities, faced quite different levels of support at their universities, had smaller or larger cohorts of students whom they saw as "like them," were experiencing contrasting college cultures, and whose institutions maintained divergent constructions of the "normal student." Cerri wanted to address how the broad social conditions that had shaped the lives of her informants intersected with their particular stories. She was convinced it was important to tell the stories of the individual students and was supported in her efforts by critical race theory, which she employed to good effect. Critical race theory emphasizes both the importance of representing the stories of people of color and the centrality of racism in American society. Cerri described the problem as she saw it:

> The inequality of social locations, that is, the idea that some social locations wield more power and privileges than others, impacts the lives of each individual participating in the schooling process and the impact is different for each one involved. For Black women undergraduates, their status as Black and Woman, intersecting with their social class and other social locations, make[s] their educational journeys specific. (Banks, 2004)

When Banks (2004) describes the purpose of her study, you can hear the echoes of critical race theory in its phrases:

> The purpose of this study is to invoke the voices of Black undergraduate women, from across the United States about their processes of negotiation in higher education. I want to explore their stories about education in their own words and from their own perspectives. My hope is that their words and experiences will challenge prominent notions that render them intellectually inferior and ill equipped for academic success.

She then followed with the kinds of research questions that her study would specifically explore.

Big Issues and Specific Projects

As you can see from the above three examples, each of the dissertation students knew the big issue they were interested in before they knew what the specific purpose of their study would be. Jeff Mangram, for example, did *not* start out saying to himself, "I want to interview social studies teachers for my dissertation. What should I interview them about?" Like all of the students whose work is recounted here, he first knew the topic he wanted to work on and then had to figure out the part of it he would study.

At the same time, moving from the statement of the problem to the purpose of the study is not a linear progression. While you are working on preparing your dissertation proposal, you are also reading other studies and exploring theories about how the world is organized, how power relations work, and other big ideas of our time. All this reading will affect how you think about your project.

You may decide to include the research questions in the purpose of your study. This is a good choice because it communicates to readers how you will address the project you have proposed. Jeff Mangram, for example, wrote his research questions immediately following his purpose of the study:

> In this research project, I seek to understand how social studies teachers make meaning of media and popular culture, and how they negotiate these meanings or perspectives of media and popular culture in their personal lives and in their pedagogical approaches in the classroom. My inquiry is guided by the following questions: How do social studies teachers reconcile or negotiate their likes or dislikes of media and popular culture texts with their students' choices? Which cultural and mediated representations are allowed in these teacher's rooms? Which are not? How do social studies teachers use their educational space to approach issues relating to media and popular

culture? How do social studies teachers understand and interpret ideological implications embedded in media and popular culture? (Unpublished dissertation proposal, 2005)

To get to the statement of the problem and the purpose of the study, talk about your interests with others. You want them to understand what this big issue is, you want them to find it interesting, and you want them to know how this issue looks from your perspective. Talking about your work not only provides opportunities to hear the ideas of others and test out how your ideas sound to other people; you also learn what different people and particular groups take for granted in relation to your topic. Vocabularies stimulate reactions in people, and you want to know what kind of weight the particular words you use carry.

THE LITERATURE REVIEW

The next section of the dissertation proposal can be either the literature review or the section on methods and procedures. Either section can go next, and you should base this decision on conventions at your university or on what works well for the way you have written and put together your proposal. Here, we will talk about the literature review next.

This section concerns how the project you plan relates to the work others have done on the topic. What ways of thinking, approaches, and frameworks will you draw on to make sense of this issue? The literature review in a dissertation is the topic of the next chapter, and there is much more discussion there of how to frame such a chapter. You should write the literature review in a dissertation proposal when you are immersed in the process of discovering the literature rather than when you have completed the work. As we said earlier, this is because you are not certain about what literature will be the most relevant. For example, after conducting most of her fieldwork, Cerri Banks, whose dissertation topic concerned the narratives of Black female university students, decided that part of the cultural capital that the students brought with them that countered some of their poor academic preparation was a "sociological imagination" (Mills, 1959), so she needed to do more of a literature review on this topic. Yet, even though she had known when she started the research that Bourdieu's concept of cultural capital was central to her work (e.g., Bourdieu, 1977), she did not realize until near the end of data collection that she wanted her dissertation to contribute to the theoretical discussion of the meanings of cultural capital. Therefore, she needed to become much more familiar with discussions of and debate about Bourdieu's theory of cultural capital. So her literature reviews for the proposal and for the dissertation were dissimilar. This is more common than not in qualitative research dissertations. Certainly, the length of the literature review depends on your certainty that the way you have framed your dissertation will remain stable. In some fields where students do qualitative dissertations, it is expected that your literature review will discuss the relevant literature in the field and state clearly how your work contributes to "the field." For other students, however, particularly those who are doing interdisciplinary work, it is not always quite so clear what "the field" is, and therefore one task of the literature review for the proposal is to actually construct an account of "the field" as you know it. Students sometimes feel that they are cobbling together a field from work on theory and drawing together multiple literatures.

Linda Steet (1993), for example, wrote a dissertation on the representation of Arabs in the photographs of *National Geographic*. She looked at *National Geographic* as an example of popular culture, but she was interested in using the lenses of multiculturalism and critical theory to frame her project. Literatures on popular culture, representation, cultural studies, multicultural education, and difference were all part of her literature review.

METHODS AND PROCEDURES

This section answers several important questions. How will you actually carry out this research? Why is the chosen method one that will facilitate gathering the kind of data that will illuminate your research question? Methods and procedures are two different sorts of methodological concerns. *Methods* refers to the research method you have chosen and allows you to comment on how qualitative methods work, why your approach fits with your topic, and the specific kind of qualitative approach you will take. *Procedures* refers to the actual steps you will take to secure informants, develop rapport, confront any problems you foresee, and determine what you will observe if you are doing participant observation. In this chapter, you might explain how some of your choices depend on your preliminary fieldwork. For example, a student who was interviewing older women about their experiences with domestic violence expected that her informants would talk about their family of choice when she asked a question about the abuse they had experienced. When the informants interpreted her question as referencing family of origin, she realized she had made assumptions that she needed to address. This is a good example of the kinds of issues this section might discuss.

This section is also a good place to discuss some of the methodological issues that arise because of your own particular social location. One student, for example, was doing a study of lesbian women who work in a
masculine-identified occupation. She observed and interviewed different
women who work in this field. As she herself was an out lesbian, she had
expected that the informants would speak much more freely with her than
they did. Her anticipation that being a member of the in-group she was
studying would enable better and earlier rapport was frustrated during
the first months of her study. This kind of example also contributes to a
discussion of methods and procedures.

The methods and procedures section should demonstrate that you
understand the method you are using to understand people's lives. It should
also illustrate that you have had some experience with the method and with
the kinds of informants you want to investigate in your study (if not the
actual informants themselves). It should describe clearly for the reader how
you are going to do the work in the field and, if you know already, what
kind of software package you will use to analyze the data. And it should
show that you have some sense of what kinds of issues you may have to
confront in the field.

ORGANIZATION

The next section of your dissertation proposal should discuss the dissertation itself. If you did not yet list and describe the research questions, you
should write about them here. If you know or have an idea about how you
will organize the chapters, it is important to sketch these out for the readers
because advice from your committee members about how you are concep-
tualizing your work is more useful if it is more specific. When the committee members know the subjects of your proposed chapters, they see how
you are thinking of categorizing your material and they can help you con-
firm the implications of these choices. Qualitative dissertations are frequently organized thematically, so you might discuss the three themes that
you suspect will ground each of the three data chapters that qualitative
dissertations usually have. To offer a realistic discussion of chapters, you
have to have collected enough data and be clear enough about your topic
to be able to forecast this.

An alternative to discussing the three themes is to describe what you
want your dissertation to cover. This coverage can include topics, perspectives, informants, and approaches. You might think, for example, that you
will devote each chapter to a particular kind of informant in order to tell
your story. In a case study of a legal advocacy center, for example, you

might devote one chapter to the perspectives of the lawyers, one to those of the clients, and one to those of the staff. You may not know when you are writing the proposal what the argument of the dissertation will be, but you may know that you want to make sure that each of these perspectives is represented. Or, if you are doing discourse analysis of how a school district deals with No Child Left Behind, you might know that you will have one chapter that analyzes the legislation and its representation in the press, one chapter that examines how the vocabulary of the policies emerge in teacher talk, and one chapter that emerges from your participation in four urban classrooms. The more you can discuss the organization of your dissertation (without faking it), the better the discussions about your work you can have with your advisor and committee.

CONCLUDING SECTION

The conclusion of the proposal includes a short discussion of (1) the limitations of your work and (2) its significance. The limitations refer to the actual limitations of your study, not another study that you did not do. If you are interviewing Chinese American immigrant women and your study includes only women from the Northeast, then one of your study's limitations may be that Chinese American women from major western cities with large Chinese American populations are excluded. You do not have to argue that it is a limitation that you did not do participant observation with these women. That would be another study, and you can describe the benefits of such research in the implications section of your dissertation's concluding chapter. If you are doing a study of a group of college women who are juniors and seniors and who have formed a group to support freshman and sophomore women of color, it is not a limitation that you are not studying white women. Here, a limitation might be that you were only able to interview the upperclasswomen, not the younger students.

No one can do a study that accounts for everything. The "limitations of the dissertation" is shorthand for this. You explain that you understand what your work enabled you to see and what its limitations are. You are not criticizing your own work in the limitations section. Rather, you are helping the reader to read the material as you want it read.

The section on the significance of your work answers questions about its importance: Who cares or should care about what you are investing so much energy in? This is where you can comment about what makes your work different from other work done in your area. Some writers emphasize how different their work is from what has already been done in order to stress the significance of this new work. This is difficult to do because writing about your work is different from talking about it. In writing, you can easily appear arrogant or seem like you are overstating your accomplishments. However, there are occasions when you are not exaggerating your contribution. When Bob Bogdan and Steve Taylor (1994) wrote a book containing the life stories of two people with intellectual disabilities, it was the first time anyone had interviewed people labeled mentally retarded and provided them space to talk about how their lives looked to them. When you are doing something innovative, this may be a moment to strongly differentiate your work from that of others.

Another strategy is to connect your research to other work that has been done, emphasizing what you are contributing to a burgeoning field rather than distancing yourself from it. This is also an important way to talk about significance, and it works well when you are doing work in a rapidly expanding area. Kristen Luschen (2005), for example, did a dissertation on sex education at a time when it was a very popular topic. The originality came from its emphasis on adults who wanted high school students who had had children or who were sexually involved at a young age to succeed. She chronicled the complicated tension between these adults' strong intention to provide an alternative view for the young women they served and their failure to do so. By looking at three educational spaces within one district, her study provided a complex representation of the struggle between institutions and individuals. She examined the negotiation between institutional policy (like the district's contraceptive distribution policy), curriculum (the progressive sex education curriculum), culture (in which distinctions were made between educators and their authority), and educators' ideas about what students' sexual health needs are and how best to attend to them in an educational context. This is a more connective way to talk about significance. If your dissertation contributes information that was not previously known—perhaps about sign language professionals or welfare-to-work programs—this section is the perfect place to describe it. Your dissertation might also have methodological significance, and you want to make sure to emphasize this as well. Remember that you are addressing all of these issues in 20 to 30 pages, so we are not suggesting deep essays on these points.

COMMON QUESTIONS ABOUT THE PROPOSAL

Should You Use Data from Fieldwork or from Textual Analysis in the Proposal?

Yes, but only a small amount. You must make sure that you, as the writer, have a strong presence in the proposal, and since the proposal is pretty short, you don't want to take up too much of those precious pages with data. A limited amount of data can be effective in showing that your project and your informants' words, or policy texts or television drama transcripts, address the same point. Another valuable use for a data segment is as an introduction to your proposal. If you start with your informants' words, and your informants' words are engaging, you bring the reader into the proposal and heighten interest in your work.

Should You Talk About Difficulties or Complications in Your Project?

Yes, because when you do so, you show your knowledge of the field and your own sophistication as a researcher. It is not necessarily a sign of the strength of your project that you gain entry with ease, face no problems with rapport, gather data easily and quickly, and leave the field with few recriminations. Sometimes the more difficult projects are challenging and therefore capable of making huge contributions to the field. When you describe these complications and your strategies for handling them, you may enable the reader to think in new ways about fieldwork. Talking about difficulties is different from being pessimistic about them. Pessimism may deflate readers whom you want to draw into, not detach from, your work. If you think of complications as being an ordinary part of research rather than a significant and unusual deterrent, then you will put yourself in a frame of mind that will allow you to represent them that way.

How Much Research Should You Do First?

As we said earlier, it is useful to have between one-fourth and one-third of your data already collected before you write a proposal. This amount of data allows you to know what you are writing about and that the topic you are interested in is actually possible to study at the site you have chosen. It is impossible to write a proposal for a qualitative study without doing any of the research because you need to know more about the outcome of the negotiation process between you and your informants. In this process, you, as the researcher, enter the field with questions to research, but you are influenced by your informants in what can be seen as a process of negotiation about how these questions have meaning for your informants. So, you usually shift your questions so that they have meaning in the particular field you're entering.

What kind of data collection is possible before proposal writing? Your department may have a hard-and-fast rule that you may only collect data after you have defended your proposal. While this is difficult for the qualitative doctoral student, you can work to overcome it by working on your project in your qualitative methods courses, through independent study projects, or as a part of your coursework.

Sometimes you are interested for your dissertation project in an event that is occurring at a particular time or in a particular place (say, while you are abroad), and you must collect all of your data before you write the proposal. This is a more difficult situation for dissertation committee members because it effectively terminates the contribution they can make to the design of the study. Sometimes, however, it is unavoidable. Flexibility is important for the qualitative proposal.

CHAPTER 6

The Chapters

When you have friends over for dinner, each phase of the evening accomplishes different purposes. You serve juice, beer, soda, or wine and tidbits at the beginning so that people get to know each other and you have time to cook. You and your guests sit down to a meal together so that people can have deeper conversations. These cultural practices guide the evening from greeting to leave-taking. We don't need to extend this metaphor too far, but the idea is the same with a dissertation.

Each of the chapters in a dissertation has a different and specific purpose. Like the new guest who needs introductions and attention, the reader of the dissertation needs to be nurtured as well, not to "have a good time," as the guest at a dinner (although it would be good if the reader enjoyed your dissertation), but to understand the dissertation as you intend it to be understood. This chapter addresses the functions that each chapter in your dissertation serves in order for it to have the effect that you want. In the introduction, you welcome readers to the text and let them know what concerns the dissertation will address. The literature review describes the conversation that your dissertation research is a part of. The methods and procedures chapter explains how you understand the research process and what you actually did to carry out the scholarship. The three data chapters each take up a different aspect of the research. The conclusion not only reminds readers of what you accomplished but also provides an opportunity to expand on your findings, describe how they should be applied, and comment on what further work researchers might do.

Some people find it helpful to sketch out these chapters on sheets of paper or set up separate computer files for each. One person who had completed her dissertation in sociology explained that she had labeled sheets of paper "Introduction," "Literature Review," "Methods and Procedures," and so on, then spread the sheets of paper on a long desk. During a 2-week period she would jot down ideas, topics, and texts that would be appropriate to include in the chapters. By the end of 2 weeks, she had a lot of scribbling, some second thoughts, but also information for developing her work. She used her proposal to flesh out these chapters, turning the scribbling into a more formal "layout."

These different chapters, taken together, work to pull the reader into your work, get and hold their interest, and demonstrate how your particular project is connected to and different from similar work or research. They cement your authority and trustworthiness as a reliable narrator. In the rest of this chapter we'll address these different sections and effects. First, we want to talk both about the order in which you should write the chapters and how to construct yourself as a reliable narrator.

WHAT SHOULD YOU WRITE FIRST?

It is a weekend night. You want to go to the movies. What should you see? You open the newspaper and see that two new films appeal to you. After reading the brief write-ups, you can say what the films are about, but you don't know any more about them. After you see a film, obviously, you know not only the plot and topic but also what world the film imagines and how the actors perform their roles—you can talk about it using specific examples. You need to see it before you can talk about it as a particular film.

Think of this as a metaphor for dissertation writing. If you know that the introduction literally introduces the reader to the project, you have to know what you actually said (in your data chapters) in order to introduce it. Our advice is to write the data chapters first. This way, when you go to place your research in context (for your literature review), you know just what the "it" is that you are contextualizing and you know that for the introduction, you will be able to say just what "it" is you are introducing. You will already have partial drafts of your dissertation's first three chapters from your proposal that you can develop after you complete the discussion of your research. As you write the data chapters, you might keep notes or write short sections as you think of them and keep these in a file to use for those other chapters. Even though a certain logic suggests that you write chapters "in order," it is a mistaken logic.

THE RELIABLE NARRATOR

There is not one specific thing that you do as the narrator of the dissertation to establish your reputation as a reliable narrator. As the section on narrative authority in Chapter 2 described, there are many strategies that writers use to gain and demonstrate their authority. And you should think about which of these strategies are useful to you in relation to your data. As the author of a dissertation, you are positioned in a particular way in relation to your readers. On the one hand, as your advisor may frequently say before the defense, you know more about your topic than anyone else because you have spent more time on it. On the other hand, your committee members most likely know more about research and have more self-confidence about what they know than you do. So you are in the situation of having to demonstrate to knowledgeable people that you are reliably narrating your dissertation.

There are several ways to enhance your reliability as a narrator. First, you need to think in a specific way about the role of a narrator in a dissertation, and then work to implement it. One aspect of this role is as a coach or leader. That is, as narrator you coach, urge, and point readers to read in the way that you want them to read. Readers can be encouraged to read as if they were reading "with you." The topic you have chosen or the stance you take may require extra effort to coach the readers to see the data and your project as you want them to see it. This does not mean that they have to agree with you. They do, however, have to see the logic of your views. This means that you want them to believe what you are saying. They will believe you, or at least see the significance of your point, even if they do not agree with you if you support what you say with examples from the data, show how your work both aligns with and diverges from other research on the topic, and explain how you went about developing relationships with your informants, gathering data, handling the problems you faced in the field, and analyzing your data. Sections of this chapter address ways to do this in more detail.

Second, make sure you actually do what you say you are going to do in the dissertation. Your introduction, in other words, has to introduce the project that you present in the dissertation, not the project you wanted to do or any other project. If you frame the project that you wrote about in your three data chapters, you are encouraging the reader to read your work in the ways you want.

Third, you become a more reliable narrator if you can imagine your readers and anticipate what parts they will agree with, need coaxing about, or question. Work to picture how your writing appears in the readers' contexts. The issues we raise in the following section should be of some help in your efforts to be read as a reliable narrator.

CHAPTER 1: THE INTRODUCTION

When you are starting a trip in a city, what do you do? If you are following directions from a friend, you may go from point A to point B exactly as the friend says without having an overall view of your trip. That method of travel will get you to your destination. However, if you get lost along the way, you may have trouble getting back on track. If you are figuring out how to find the jazz club on your own, however, you will probably take out a map to see where it is in relation to where you are. You will see that you must travel east toward the center of the city, then jog north for a bit. You will see what subway to take, and you will guess how long you will have to walk once you leave the station. Before you start, in other words, you have a picture in your head about the nature of the trip. This method of travel will clearly get you to your destination, and if you make an error, you will be able to figure out how to rectify it.

An introductory dissertation chapter is like the second method of travel, but it is not a possibility; it is a necessity. The introduction has a minimum requirement that it must meet: to set up readers' expectations for what will come so that they know what the dissertation is about. What can the reader expect from this dissertation? What will the journey demand? Meet this minimum expectation, and you will not encounter complaints that the dissertation was not competently introduced. You can have a much more powerful effect on your readers, however, if you are also able to interest, engage, and tantalize them about your project.

When writing the introduction, the tendency for many dissertation writers is to impress readers with the depth of their scholarly thinking. You should do this, but you should also impress them with the quality of your writing. Do not be afraid to "grip" readers, to have a hook that makes them want to read further. You are not only introducing your topic, you are also introducing your style of writing and your voice. Here, you should be developing the tone of your dissertation and showing readers how they should read your work. Establishing a voice is something that will develop as you write your dissertation, but it should be initiated in the introduction.

Think of the introduction as an essay of around 15 pages. It may be quite a bit longer, but it should not be shorter. The introduction explains the large problem, of which your research addressed one part; offers the reader an explanation of how you approached the project and why; and perhaps introduces you as a researcher (e.g., why you got interested in this project, your relationship to it, what way of thinking—theory—frames the way you either approached the project in the beginning or came to see it as you analyzed your data). You may describe the amount of time you spent in the field, any significant problems you faced, and—briefly—how your work relates to other research in this area (or why there is not any or only very little research in this area). The last part of the introduction previews what each following chapter contains.

How do you both describe the project so that your readers' expectations fit what follows and grab their interest so that they want to read further? Here are a few ideas about how to approach the task. Look at these as examples of possibilities, not as a description of the only options.

The Direct Approach

In the direct approach, you tell the reader what the dissertation is about, why it is a significant problem to investigate, and what aspect of the problem—that is, the purpose of your specific study—you took up. You may use phrases such as "This is a study of . . ." or "This research addresses the question of. . . . It argues that. . . ." This approach may not be sophisticated. It may not entice readers to continue of their own accord, but it does give them a map of what is to come, and it stabilizes the research, establishing your authority as a narrator. You may use this strategy in the first draft, just to make sure that you say clearly what your project studies and how it approaches the topic, but this is certainly adequate for a final draft as well. It is not elegant, but it is perfectly adequate.

The Historical Opening

You can inform readers of the longstanding nature of the problem by presenting it in historical context. While not useful for all topics (especially if yours does not have a long history or if the history is not relevant), the historical opening offers the reader the opportunity to see that you have tackled a big problem, that it has been approached in many ways over the years, and that you will show how your way of thinking about it offers some originality. In a dissertation on sex workers in Amsterdam, for example, the introductory paragraph opened like this:

> Documentation of prostitution in the Netherlands dates back to the 1500s. Even at that time, local city and State officials tolerated concentrations of this type of commercial activity in most mercantile centers. Although the practice remained stigmatized in the centuries that followed, the commercial exchange of sex for money became public in window-brothels within consigned places such as the Red Light District. State regulation of prostitution as an institution, rather than a de facto practice, began to occur during the 1700s when the French occupied the Netherlands. (Gregory, 2003)

After more historical discussion, her dissertation then described the "windows" where prostitutes advertise their services and explained what contribution her research made to the discussion of sex workers in countries where this kind of labor is regulated and legal. This form of introduction is not suitable for a historical dissertation, but it works well for a topic that has a long history and is being investigated from sociological, anthropological, or psychological perspectives.

It's in the News

If your dissertation topic is considered a current social problem, another introductory approach emphasizes its significance by demonstrating how, whichever way citizens turn, this problem confronts them because of its heavy media coverage. Kristen Luschen (2005) studied sex education, and while most of the treatment of it in recent years had focused on abstinence education, she could point to its coverage in such national newspapers as *The New York Times, The Chicago Tribune, The Los Angeles Times,* and *The Washington Post* to emphasize its significance as a topic and to discuss how policy decisions about funding sex education were currently regulated. Linda Waldron (2002) studied how teachers and students in public schools understood school violence in the aftermath of the Columbine killings. An important part of her introductory chapter examined the huge media coverage of Columbine and how difficult it would have been for school district officials, parents, and students to avoid the discussions, since they took place on all the local television stations. This approach in her introduction enabled her to argue that school violence was on people's minds.

It Goes Against Common Sense

Qualitative methods make strong contributions when they frame a project in a way that does not seem obvious at first glance. A good introductory strategy might be to compare the perspective that your research takes on a topic with the prevailing approaches or those that are most popular in current policy. This approach can be slightly dangerous if you exaggerate the differences, but it can work well if you frame this in an understated way. Janet Dodd, for example, is currently looking not at the benefits of feminism for legal changes around sexual violence but at the dangers of how legal language has watered down significant ideas and made them contradictory. Lesley Bogad's (2002) study of young people who saw themselves contributing to social change demonstrated how their behaviors reinforced the status quo. Here is the opening paragraph of Amy Best's (1998) dissertation on the prom:

> Typically, the high school prom is represented as a place to have fun, to celebrate their emerging adulthood, to act as well-dressed grownups for a few brief hours. But high school proms are also sites of cultural and political

struggle and conflict. One school was set ablaze in an attempt to prevent interracial dating at the prom, students have sued their schools to attend the prom with same sex partners, African American students have protested their proms because of the music played, and schools have imposed rules requiring that the crowning of the prom queen alternate yearly between Black female students and white female students. While these examples are extreme, there is no doubt that the prom is a site where practices of gender, race, sexuality and social class are produced, sustained and, at times, contested. (p. 12)

The tone of such an approach might be represented in the phrase "You might think that X is true. But in this project I show that in fact Y is the case."

The Vignette

If you have a story from your fieldnotes or from an interview transcript that raises issues that the rest of the dissertation explores, you might consider using it as an opening to the introductory chapter. This is a way of getting the reader's attention and starting off in a more inductive manner. The example offers readers a chance to consider what they make of the story you tell in their own engagement with it before you frame it for them from your time in the field and your theoretical understanding. There are always stories in qualitative fieldwork, but you have to be able to draw meaning from them to employ this strategy. You may also tell a story from your data, using your informants' words or notes taken from participant observation. Here is an example of what such an opening might look like:

> When Charlotte Younger attended an urban high school, she was a high-performing white student who took many Advanced Placement (AP) classes. One of her friends, Ruby, an African American student, who, Charlotte said, later went on to attend an Ivy League university, wanted to take Modern European History, one of these AP classes, during their junior year. The teacher did not think that Ruby had the grades in earlier history classes for this "so-called highly competitive" class. Charlotte said that this experience affirmed "how tracked my school was. I saw lots of Black students in the hallways, but rarely in my classes. And this was an urban school." When Ruby and Ruby's mother complained to the principal, the teacher was pressured to admit her. "That was an eye-opening experience!" Charlotte said. This dissertation examines perspectives of students like Charlotte and Ruby in a tracked urban high school in the northeast. It traces the raced experiences of

12 Black and 11 white students in their classes at the school over their junior and senior years.

Here the narrator tells a story that represents the focus of the dissertation.

Whichever of these approaches you employ, it is simply one of many ways you will use to influence how your readers approach and understand your work. So make sure that early in the introduction you state clearly what your dissertation is about. Then, when you describe why this is an important problem, or why your approach is different from others, or how your research connects with work that has been done, your reader will know what is being compared or contrasted or contextualized. A good rule of thumb is to make certain that you mention exactly what your project is about within the first 3 pages of the introduction; usually, the sooner the better. Here's why this works well. When you describe competing ways scholars or activists have traditionally considered an issue, for example, you want to make sure that the readers know why you want them to know about this. If they know exactly what your project is, they will realize why you are explaining a particular part of the background.

CHAPTER 2: THE LITERATURE REVIEW

A literature review often seems daunting to doctoral students. Imagine it, however, as a description of the conversation that already exists in relation to your project. Your assignment is to describe the conversation to the committee. You might approach your topic in a way that fits comfortably with how others understand "the field." In this case, you do not have to work too hard to frame the structure of the conversation. There will be plenty of dialogue, arguments, and studies that build on one another already in existence. But other topics and approaches require more work to frame that conversation because you are not walking into a module already constructed. In this case, your task is to explain why the conversation you construct is a legitimate one.

Regarding the literature review, one doctoral student in sociology said he pretended that members of his dissertation committee were lazy but really interested in his topic. They wanted to know the "ins and outs" of the dissertation topic but did not want to read all the books and articles about it. So he said that he gave them the topic "in a nutshell." That nutshell was about 30 pages long, but it discussed the major themes, issues, and findings involving his topic.

Another doctoral student imagined the literature review in a party scenario. When another guest came up to her and asked, "So what do you do?" she would respond by telling the guest the topic of her dissertation. Interested, the person wanted to know everything about the topic, but since they were at a party, she needed to explain it rather quickly. Her explanation also had to be interesting, in order to keep the person's attention. The language would have to be clear, the points made well. She would have to give a broad overview that did not ignore the interesting contradictions and complexities of the topic.

Regardless of what mental strategy you use, your tasks for the literature review should include the following:

1. Make the topic interesting for the reader.
2. Teach the reader something new about the topic.
3. Avoid the "list effect."
4. Include descriptions and analyses of the literature (not just summaries). In other words, review from a point of view.
5. Highlight trends as well as inconsistencies in the literature.
6. Make an argument to help the reader draw conclusions about the literature.
7. Point out how your work both differs from and connects to the literature you describe in your review.

The literature review should not just be a chore that you must undertake; it should help you in several ways. Knowing what other scholars have written about your dissertation topic helps you better understand how the topic has been analyzed, what has been said about it, and what more needs to be said. The "what more needs to be said" can be the driving force of your dissertation.

Sometimes people get caught up in the "list effect" we mentioned earlier when writing a literature review. What this means is that the dissertation writer organizes the literature around the authors of the books and articles that are being reviewed. Here, the reader comes upon paragraph after paragraph or sentence after sentence beginning with some version of "According to Smith (1999) . . . ," whereupon the writer lists the scholars and their major findings, using transitional phrases between each entry in the list. While this may be a great strategy for an annotated bibliography, it makes for boring literature reviews. While not a foolproof way of preventing the problem, you can avoid the list effect by organizing your literature review around themes and major findings. You may change your strategy or organization structure at times. For example, you may start by discussing the classic early-20th-century writing that was done in your field and the findings of the initial major scholars. This may be discussed in historical terms, referring to the literature and to the historical influences that shaped it. Or this historical approach may cover only the last 40 or 50 years. From here, you may discuss more recent findings that are organized around themes or according to various inconsistencies or contradictions in the literature. You may also discuss how different forms of literature (scholarly books and articles, popular magazines, television commentary, Internet sources) have addressed your topic. Regardless of your strategy, you want to make sure that you are not creating a list that follows any set pattern from beginning to end (writer 1 wrote A, writer 2 wrote B, writer 3 wrote C, etc.).

One of the purposes of the literature review is for students to demonstrate the breadth of their knowledge. Doctoral students have to show their knowledge of the topic and that they did a close reading of the literature available on the topic. This is frequently a humbling experience. You are not the only person writing on the topic, and most topics have been discussed in great detail, sometimes by scholars who are very good researchers and writers. Even if you are critical of the work other researchers have done on the topic you are researching, you need to demonstrate your familiarity with it.

One effective way to demonstrate this familiarity is to explicate the author's work before you critique it. Explication is a way of showing respect for the work the author has done, and it shows you capable of careful and close reading. Explications for qualitative studies might address the following questions: Using the author's words, what is the argument? Why does the argument take the form that it does? What are "the sides"? What is at stake? How do the authors represent themselves in the text? How are data displayed and organized? What is the research design? How does the author represent decisions about methods? You would not provide this much detail about every text in your literature review, but you would give major work this sort of serious attention. Even with explication, there is room for critique. Critique demonstrates your analysis on the material and is a significant part of your review.

The literature review shows readers how you relate to a group of people who have connected in some way with the same topic you have. They may have approached it differently, or addressed the same issue but with a different sample, or used such different conceptual frames that the problem addressed does not appear the same, and so on. There is an "academic conversation" going on around you, and the literature review demonstrates to your committee how you frame the conversation, how you see your place in this conversation, and your relationship to the other participants.

CHAPTER 3: METHODS AND PROCEDURES

Methods and procedures connect to each other, but they do not refer to the same thing. A method is about the big picture. It answers such questions as: What does this approach get you? How does this approach frame a question? How does it understand a problem? How did it lead you, guide you, and shape the work that you did? *Methods* is a term that refers to how qualitative methods approach research. It means that this section must illustrate how your form of qualitative method—in-depth interviewing, participant observation, institutional ethnography, feminist methods—approaches the research process and how it frames the world. DeVault (1999) refers to this as a discussion of methodology. A procedure positions you on your particular part of the canvas. It is a discussion of the specific decisions you made, the actual problems you faced in the field. It is the place where you describe how you got access to the site or to informants, how you established rapport, how you collected data, and what specifically happened when you did fieldwork. Coding data is also a procedural question. It is the place where you describe the kind of qualitative software program you used (if you did) as well as how and when you incorporated theoretical approaches (e.g., grounded theory, postpositivism) in your analysis. It is where you describe the mistakes you made and their effects, in your judgment, on your research.

You help the reader make sense of your understanding of your approach and how you undertook your scholarship if you separate methods and procedures into different sections. You usually begin with a discussion of the particular qualitative method that you chose and how it frames knowledge, human relationships, and the big questions in life. Even in this section, you should refer to your own work so that it is not just a discussion of qualitative methods in general. Rather, this part of the chapter clearly places your work in a qualitative framework and shows how you understand that framework. Of course, in order to do this you need to know the literature about methods. Just as there is literature about your topic, there is literature about your methods. In most fields, there are journals that tend to publish articles specifically about methods. You should know these journals and know the types of articles they have published and what has been written in them about the methods you use. You need to know the method literature well and know the major authors who have developed and employed the methods, the significant issues and developments related to the methods, and the controversies that may surround the methods you use.

Qualitative studies often employ different methods. Especially if you are writing an interdisciplinary dissertation, you may use more than one research method. These may include historiography, policy analysis, genealogy, discourse analysis, semistructured interviews, participant observation, textual analysis, and others. When describing your methods, state why you chose these methods and their importance for your research.

In the section on procedures, which usually follows a discussion of methods, you want to communicate to the reader the actual decisions you made and the specifics you encountered every step of the way. The reader can then come to an understanding about your work—processes, decisions, encounters in the field, and so on. The procedures section helps show the reader how you made the method your own. As a novice, you might think that mistakes that you made are things to be covered up. But the opposite is true. There is no "perfect" field project where the researcher always made the right decision and where nothing went wrong. Even if there were, qualitative researchers understand that being in the field involves the researcher in a messy process of having to make spur-of-the-moment decisions and of having informants who get ill, change their mind, and so on. It is why qualitative researchers stay in the field for a long time: We are looking for patterns over time, not making judgments based on isolated or snap decisions. As you write about your problems or mistakes, you may have a great contribution to make to the literature in the field. Perhaps your error led you to see something that you would not have otherwise. Perhaps a mistake you made enabled you to see how important something was to your informants that you otherwise would not have realized. In one dissertation project, for example, the researcher was interviewing a high school dropout who was just finishing her GED. The informant had been describing her interest in school before she dropped out, her family's lack of support for her education, and the tension she felt juggling these two contradictory pulls on her. The interviewer said to her, "You sound so introspective about your situation." The informant did not know what the word *introspective* meant, and she stopped speaking in such a flowing manner. Clearly, the interviewer had not been thoughtful enough about how she responded to the informant, and her bad choice of words shut down her informant. At the same time, even though this was a mistake, the researcher learned how much the woman felt the effects of her stymied education and how aware she was of the cultural capital she lacked. Writing about that in the methods chapter was important.

If you are unsure about how to think about the methods and procedures chapter, here are some questions that might help you organize your thinking and writing about it:

1. What expectations exist for you for discussing method in your dissertation? How do you know this? How have these expectations

been communicated to you? Different universities have specific traditions for handling this chapter, and you need to make certain that you understand how things work on your campus.

2. How would you describe the keywords of ethnographic method (i.e., the vocabulary qualitative methodologists use to discuss common practices, perspectives, and problems)? Working on this question may help you write the section on methodology (see Atkinson, Coffey, & Delamont, 2003).

3. Describe a methodological insight you gained while doing your research.

4. What "rules" of method have you "broken" or "bent" and to what effect?

One way to think about this chapter is to imagine yourself teaching the reader something new about methods. Many articles about methodological issues are drawn from writers' dissertation chapters on methods and procedures. Some examples will show how the actual decisions a researcher made, the worries or feelings they had while doing the research, or the problems they encountered can help readers think differently about methodological concerns. Several writers have discussed how their assumptions in their dissertations about the sufficiency of their skin color or ethnic identity for establishing rapport in the field with informants who shared these characteristics were overcome when differences, such as class or age, proved more powerful than they thought (De Andrade, 2000; Nelson, 1996). Another methodological text discussed how the dissertation writer struggled with her identity as a researcher in a classroom when the teacher kept trying to make her show more authority than she felt would allow her to establish rapport with the students (Lareau, 1989; see also Thorne, 1993).

Naturally, not every dissertation has a paradigm-shifting or earth-shattering "something new" in its methods section. What you teach readers may be subtle. It may be a reminder about the importance of mixing methods, it may show them a way of altering interviews in order to make them more effective in difficult circumstances (such as when interviewing individuals who cannot speak), it may teach them about a method that is used in another discipline but not well known in your field (such as literary deconstruction for those in education), or it may describe how qualitative and quantitative methods are combined. Of course, there is always the opportunity of creating a paradigm shift in research methods or of discovering a new method, but in most cases method sections should teach readers about the importance of your research method for the type of research you are doing and why this research method is significant. In so doing, you should highlight in your writing the actual work you did as you employed your methods.

CHAPTERS 4, 5, AND 6: THE DATA CHAPTERS

There is no doubt that your data chapters are central to your dissertation. Even if your other chapters are strong, the good dissertation depends on strong data in the three central chapters and on their representation. We say here that in the qualitative dissertation there should usually be three data chapters, each of which examines a different theme or takes up a different aspect of the narrative you construct about your research. But this is not always the case. Sometimes two data chapters are adequate or nothing less than five will suffice (see Kliewer, 1995; Solomon, 1999). Since the expectation at most universities is that three data chapters can provide an adequate account of your research, you must have a good reason for going in a different direction. There is nothing about the qualitative approach that absolutely demands three data chapters, but the consensus that seems to exist on campuses that this is the case is powerful. Be aware of this when making a decision.

State Your Argument

Qualitative dissertations are evidence-based texts, so central to your decision about how to organize the data chapters must be how to showcase your data and use them to the best effect for your argument. When you are trying to decide what to put in these chapters, in other words, you want to make sure that you make good use of your data, that you make them look good, and that you harness your data's energy for the story you want to tell.

The first question you ask yourself when it comes to organizing your data chapters should be: What is the story you want to tell? Your work on data analysis both helps you to get to that story and aids in dividing the material into the chapters. When you ask yourself about the story you are telling, you should write an answer to that question that begins with the phrase "This is a story about. . . ." And then you complete the sentence. As you work on this sentence, you need to revise it until it tells a definitive story. Another way to put this is to say that you are developing an argument. One method you might use to push yourself toward naming the story you will tell is to write a second sentence that begins with the phrase "This dissertation argues that. . . ." Put these two sentences together, continue to refine them, and you should be able to develop a dissertation that is not only "about something" but that also takes a specific stance on it. Here are some examples, taken from some dissertation projects, of how this might work.

Taking an example from Jennifer Esposito's (2002) dissertation, *Lotions and Potions: The Meanings College Women Make of Everyday Practices of Femininities*, the two sentences would look something like this:

> This is a story about how femininity forms a significant part of the "hidden curriculum" of college life. The dissertation argues that informants must become students of the feminine in order to decide how they will "fit in" to a consumer-oriented campus culture. The multiple sources they used to learn about femininity yielded conflicting messages, so college women must negotiate competing desires.

This exercise might look like the following if we use Lesley Bogad's (2002) dissertation, *Feed Your Mind: A Qualitative Study of Youth, Power and Privilege*, as the text:

> This is a story of a group of young, middle-class, almost entirely white adolescents and their experiences in a weekly discussion group they attend before their public high school starts. The dissertation argues that these students continually negotiate the tension between a strong commitment to social justice, a perspective that they clearly articulate, and their roots in an ideology of individualism that suggests that individual success is primarily up to one's own efforts. They have much more difficulty naming this perspective, and hence it generally remains invisible to them, reaffirming their privilege.

Here is another example to show what these sentences might look like, using the dissertation of Chris Kliewer (1995), who followed 10 children with the label of Down syndrome in nine different classrooms for 5 years to understand inclusion and the meaning of Down syndrome in different contexts:

> This is a story of how different discourse communities socially construct children with the label of Down syndrome. The dissertation argues that, contrary to the traditional professional definition that equates it with mental retardation, Down syndrome is multiply represented by different groups and is a "complex series of shifting unstable social constructions." Some teachers could represent

students with Down syndrome as competent because they interpreted things the students did "not as evidence of cognitive defi-
ciencies, but rather as communication and movement differences
that resulted in difficulties negotiating the children's classrooms."

You may not be able to state the argument cogently at first, but working on this exercise will help you to do so. As you work up these two sentences, you are forced to think of what your chapters need to do to make
this argument strong. What does each chapter need to contain in order to
build the evidence for your argument?

Organize Your Data

In addition to bolstering the argument that you want to make, other issues
influence your choices about how to divide up the chapters. The kind of
data you have, the way you want to tell your story, the contribution you
want to make—these all offer resources for organization. Here we describe
some of the most common choices that doctoral students make to organize
the chapters.

Thematic Organization. Qualitative researchers frequently talk
about their findings in terms of themes, that is, ideas around which data
cluster that have emerged from work with informants. Because qualitative
researchers tend to see themselves as inductive researchers, they frequently
speak of themes that data promote. A common strategy is to organize each
chapter around a different theme. If you choose this approach, keep thinking about how it will contribute to your larger argument.

Data-Type Organization. If your dissertation employs an eclec-
tic approach, making use of different methods and forms of data collection, another choice is to organize your chapters according to the kind of
data you write about. Casella (1997) took this approach, dividing up his
chapters according to whether the data were historical, notes from participant observation and interviews, or textual analysis. If you study how audiences make sense of particular visual texts, such as television or film, this
can be a useful approach: You might have a chapter on the texts, a chapter
on the production efforts surrounding these texts, and a chapter on how
particular audience members make sense of them. McGowan (2001) took
an approach like this in her study of soap operas.

Chronological Organization. If you have done a case study or
even a multisited study (Marcus, 1998) over time, you might organize your

chapters chronologically. Here, you emphasize the beginning, middle, and end of the particular narrative you want to construct. Solomon's (1999) dissertation about poor women on welfare who were training to become nursing aides took this form. She started with the barriers these women faced in going to class and keeping up with the work. She stayed with the women throughout the class (actually, with three groups of women), exploring how the class constructed knowledge, how the women engaged with the educational and pedagogical issues in the classes, and how the teacher understood and treated these students. She then followed the students into their practical training during their internships in nursing homes. She looked at how the women formed relationships with each other over time, using these relationships to support one another and to help face the concerns that arose in the classes. She examined the ideas of professionalism that the students developed. Finally, she followed them into the workforce, at least those who got into the workforce. As you can see, this approach uses a kind of before-during-and-after method of organization. The organization of the chapters must support the argument that is made in them; it offers a strategy that enables the evidence to be marshaled in a powerful way to support the argument.

A common sociological chronological scheme that is a useful organizational tool depends on the idea of a career. Defined by Howard Becker (1970), it means the series of steps that people take for participation in a particular way of life. It documents the stages of involvement. It also refers to how you take on a particular identity or how that identity changes over time. Very different from the traditional definition of *career* as it is related to the professions, this form of "career" can be used to trace the changes in anyone's life over time, including drug users, encyclopedia salespersons, people with autism who use facilitated communication, belly dancers, school dropouts, college sophomores, ebay users, and so on. This approach is chronological because it depends on the idea of stages to divide up experience. It is also democratic because anyone can have one.

Classificatory Organization. Another effective way of approaching the organization of your chapters involves developing a classification scheme, dividing your data into categories. In this approach, you show the reader how the topic is composed of multiple categories. Your definitions of these categories and the evidence you provide both frame and illustrate your story. Categorizing can be a powerful tool for analyzing the issues. There are multiple forms of classification. The taxonomy is a system, or scheme, of classification. If you use a taxonomy for organization, different chapters can be devoted to the specific categories you discuss. You might classify forms of educational travel, kinds of talk that dominate a setting, the scheme a magazine uses to categorize photos of particular ethnic populations, or the sorting scheme people use to organize family photographs. Another classification, or categorical, approach could examine the kinds of discourses that support and structure situations; some examples include one dissertation that classified discourses about school violence that inform public schooling (Waldron, 2002) and another that categorized discourses of parent involvement in a public high school (Bannister, 2001). A dissertation might also classify the kinds of players or actors involved in a particular site, event, or institution or the various perspectives that are central to an institution or public event. The categorizing, or classifying, approach works well when breaking down a whole into its parts in order to provide insight into the story you want to tell.

Continuum Organization. A continuum is a kind of classificatory scheme, so it could be grouped with the previous section. It is a bit looser, though, since it attempts to classify along a range. We discuss it separately because we want to alert you to the dangers of this approach. Constructing a continuum is a way of taking a whole and breaking it into parts according to a progression or sequence. *Continuum* has the same root as *continuous*, so it emphasizes connections among the parts even as it differentiates among them. If you envision a continuum as a line that stretches between two concepts, with different points on it, you would explore the relationship between the points and hence the relationship between the words at each end of the line. A continuum does not emphasize oppositions, like strong versus weak, poor versus rich, or leader versus follower. Rather, it makes an argument about why points on a line are different from each other (that is, why they are not the same point), but it centers their relationship. If a taxonomy works to differentiate the kinds of talk newly adoptive parents use to describe the adoption experience, for example, a continuum would emphasize connections between how adoptive parents talked about their first and second adoptions (see Flower-Kim, 2005). The continuum emphasizes the connections, the similarities in the parents' language about the first and second adoptions. It might also communicate some differences (e.g., "We had learned how to get around some of the requirements by the time we wanted the second child"), but it emphasizes how the two adoptions are part of a whole experience. If you decide to use a continuum to organize your dissertation, you need to know what terms are at each end of the continuum and how to differentiate the points.

One of the dangers of the continuum as an organizational scheme is that it may construct relationships as linear. Just the picture we described above of a line with points on it indicates linearity. Since most relationships are not linear, and since qualitative methods are most effective when they portray complications, you need to be especially thoughtful when you use this strategy.

These different organizational strategies do not exhaust the possibilities, but they offer you a range of ways to think about dividing up how you will talk about your data and make an argument. The form you choose will make a significant difference in the way you present data, in the shape of the dissertation, and in the manner in which the story emerges. Which approach you choose depends on your story and your data. You cannot do a taxonomy if you do not have the data to use for classification and if you did not think about your evidence in terms of types. You should not use a chronological scheme if chronology is not useful for your argument or for the story. But having choices helps you to write up your data in the strongest way.

CHAPTER 7: THE CONCLUSION

By the time most students get to the last chapter, they have about had it. They feel that they have already said everything they have to say and are fearful of repeating themselves, they are worried that they have no recommendations for further research, and they are unclear about the implications of their research for practice. If you feel this way by the time you reach this chapter, don't worry. You're not alone. But a strong conclusion is an important part of the dissertation. A weak conclusion leaves readers hanging, unsure of whether they know the importance of your work and of how your work fits into the larger scheme of things. A strong conclusion satisfies readers that you understand what you contributed in the dissertation and that you can distinguish between the less and more important aspects of your work and, therefore, what should be followed up in future research or attempted in practice. A good conclusion is worth a lot (partly because there are so few of them). A good conclusion makes committee members happy.

The ingredients for a conclusion include your summary of what you argued, the story you told, and how you narrated this story throughout your separate chapters. A good conclusion summarizes, elaborates, and reviews what you covered in each data chapter. The conclusion also includes a discussion of further research that your project suggests should be done and the implications for practice that your research suggests. You have to make the connections between your work and these implications, just as you need to explain why your research suggests further research. Be particular in these explanations.

At the same time, the conclusion is also a space for you to write in a more expansive mode about the research that you did. Because the dissertation is a place for you to demonstrate your ability to conduct research, the pressure to be more reserved is strong during most chapters. But in the conclusion, after you have closely described your findings and discussed what more can be researched and practiced, you can loosen that reserve a bit to engage in some speculation about your research or the topic, raise questions that you see as interesting, perhaps bring some passion to the topic.

The conclusion does not have to be a long chapter—8 to 10 pages often suffice. You want them to be 10 interesting pages, however, and if you don't leave time to write the conclusion, you may find yourself willing to say almost anything to finish. Avoid this situation.

We offer a couple of hints. First, it is easier to write a conclusion when you have not put the conclusion in the introduction. An introduction only needs to introduce your work. If you say too much there about what you found, you put yourself in the situation of repeating yourself in the conclusion. So you might try reading over the introduction to see if there is any concluding material there.

Second, the conclusion may be the place to relate your topic to something else. This might be an event in the news about which your work offers some insight or another aspect of the general topic you addressed that your perspective illuminates. If you studied reading teachers, for example, you could make connections to music teachers. If you studied the education of architects, you could make connections to the education of another group with whom you see a relationship or want to draw contrasts. We offer these examples somewhat arbitrarily, but the point is that you can strengthen the conclusion by trying to understand what the principles are that you analyzed and how these principles look in relation to another group.

As you can see from this chapter, all of the chapters in the dissertation share the need to be well written, thoughtful, and useful to your project. At the same time, they each serve a different purpose for the dissertation and should be distinctive in these ways. The work you do to make each chapter serve its purpose offers you an opportunity to make your dissertation a strong one.

CHAPTER 7

Writing as Work— Getting It Done

"Designing a study, doing fieldwork, analyzing the data, and writing it up"—this orderly representation of the dissertation process flows effortlessly from our lips and has entered common parlance (at least on campus). When academics speak like this, we provide a frame for new doctoral students to imagine the dissertation process, but we may also oversimplify the work of producing a dissertation (as well as construct the process as more linear than it actually is). Writing a dissertation demands from you multiple and quite different skills and attributes. Self-confidence and self-discipline might be characterized as part of your personal character traits or as habits you have developed, but they might also relate to your social location in relation to class, race, or gender. You may be self-disciplined because getting a doctorate is important for your career aspirations and for the pride it will bring to your family and community, but your self-confidence may waver because you are unfamiliar, as a first-generation college and doctoral student, with the process and level of expectation for the dissertation. Your experience as a writer might be partially influenced by your undergraduate major or your class background. Your understanding of the dissertation process might be connected to the quality of the advising you receive or to the cultural capital you bring to the university. Your level of commitment to getting a Ph.D. might be another of your personal characteristics. Finally, competing demands in your life—demands of family, work, and the like—create another set of stresses that define your particular situation. When all of these elements intersect each other, they are complicated and challenging.

This chapter addresses the work involved in writing a qualitative dissertation rather than the content. There are already a number of useful books available about writing in general, and we will refer you to these as we go along. Here, however, we will speak to the work of writing—addressing the personal, stylistic, and strategic questions that writing forces you to confront. We will discuss styles of writing as well as the issues of perseverance, self-confidence, building support, and getting it done. Finally, we will end with just a few notes about content.

THE SIGNIFICANCE OF PUBLIC EXPOSURE

Good writing demands public exposure. While putting words on the page is a private matter, in that you are sitting alone (hopefully) in front of a computer, you need to think of what you write as a malleable text that you can modify and change as you complete successive drafts. You make these modifications because you learn what readers bring to your text that influences how they make sense of your words, and you need the perspectives of different readers in order to make these changes. Dissertation writing groups, class presentations, and conference presentations move you into the public sphere. When you spend time in this sphere, you become less attached to your words (in a certain sense) because you stop seeing them as representing an evaluation of you. You see them as a way to communicate what you want to say. Spending time in the public sphere helps you see your writing not as a static product (i.e., this is what I have to say and I said it—phew!) but as a living organism that needs to be nurtured (i.e., read) by others to grow.

We actually come to see texts more like oral communication when we spend time with our writing in the public sphere. Over the years, for example, students have asked us to define different terms, such as *discourse, agency*, and the *literature review*. We offer explanations, and when these explanations do not satisfy, we develop new ones. For example, we came up with the description of the literature review as the conversation that takes place in your field of study. We only came up with this description, however, because students did not understand other ways we had of talking about this section of the dissertation. Since we were in the public sphere, we had to continually work to develop ways of defining terms when earlier definitions did not satisfy. We did not offer an explanation and then stick with it, but rather continually modified it until it answered the questions students raised about the literature review. Writing is rarely seen as casually as talk, however, so strategies like moving yourself to the public sphere that push you to increase your willingness to modify your original words benefit your work.

We have a friend who, over the years, has sent out drafts of articles and chapters as soon as they are completed. Frequently the drafts are rough, but he knows that his work will improve when others read it. Sometimes he knows he has something important to say but is not sure that he has chosen the right approach, and he depends on readers' comments to judge. Sometimes he needs assurance that he is on the right track. This practice of publicly sharing his work in draft form has meant that he has a high acceptance rate when he sends the articles to journals. He already knows how a variety of readers make sense of his work. He trusts, to use Howard Becker's (1986) language, that the readers will read his work "in the right spirit, treating as preliminary what is preliminary" (p. 21). Becker goes on to explain what he means by this spirit: "helping the author sort out the mixed-up ideas of a very rough draft or smooth out the ambiguous language of a later version, suggesting references that might be helpful or comparisons that will give the key to some intractable puzzle" (p. 21). To have this trust in your readers, you need to have a certain kind of self-confidence, and we devote the next section to it.

SELF-CONFIDENCE, CULTURAL CAPITAL, AND THE DISSERTATION PROJECT

There is a difference between having confidence that you can do good work and being full of yourself. It is easier to write when you are confident that you have something to say that others will find interesting and when you do not doubt the worth of your work. Confidence also makes it easier for you to share your work in draft form with others. Few of you will have consistent confidence, however. It probably ebbs and flows, as ours does. On days when your writing is going well, you may feel confident about your work. But on the days when you struggle, you may be filled with doubt. These shifts in feeling are part of the dissertation process, so it helps if you are not tightly up against a deadline.

Some students, in our experience, seem to have more confidence than others. We are not talking about swagger here, but a quiet sense that their work is important and that they will find a way to communicate that importance. This confidence emanates from several sources. The primary source of one student's confidence, at least from our perspective, came from her belief that she had not yet read about the lives of African American students in predominantly white settings in any way that approximated her own experiences in such schools over the years. The importance of filling this gap combined with a belief that such work would be a contribution to a community of students gave her confidence. Here, confidence emerged not only from her academic preparation but also from her commitment to social justice. She knew that she had something to say.

Having something to say is not the only source of confidence, however. Institutionally, the dissertation is a project designed to show others that you can do research competently. For some of you, this is your first major research project, and it seems to be a gigantic task, a big hurdle you must get over before you can do the things that you really want to do. Others of you may have had a sort of apprenticeship contributing research and writing to grants faculty have applied for, so while the dissertation is a big project, it is not a completely unfamiliar process to you. Having such experience gives you a kind of leg up in the process. It may also give you some confidence. Another source of self-confidence is the cultural capital that comes from family members who have higher education or doctoral degrees or simply familiarity with academic life.

It is important to acknowledge cultural capital because often it is not mentioned when we discuss dissertation writing. How much, for example, should you read when you write a dissertation? How do you find the answer to this question? Having had experience working with faculty members on grants or projects helps you to answer this kind of question. You know that no matter how smart you are, the dissertation involves a significant amount of work and that being well read is among your tasks. You are lucky if reading about your topic also gives you pleasure. Students who have watched faculty members do research and have worked with them informally learn the rules of the research game.

WRITING GROUPS FOR DISSERTATION SUPPORT

If we could, we would pass a law that all doctoral students join dissertation support groups while they were writing their dissertations. Don't worry! We can hear those of you who live far from campus, or who are single parents who also work and have no time for one more thing, responding to us, "Are you kidding? That's the straw that would break the camel's back." We have no power to enforce our scheme, but we will take the opportunity to emphasize its value. Dissertation writing support groups are important to doctoral students for many reasons. Here are some of them:

1. All of you in the group are going through the same process. You are facing pressures, expectations, advisors, fears, and anxiety—as well as excitement and hope. Talking about these issues with your support group helps you get through the dissertation process because what you experience is part of the culture rather than foreign to it. You will not all have exactly the same experience, but you will all understand the currency that energizes and feeds this culture. This is probably the more therapeutic aspect of the support group.

2. The group members constitute an important audience for your work. They will read your work closely before faculty do, and they can ask you important questions about your writing: "Is this the main point you wanted to make?" "So, this is what your dissertation is about?" "Did you mean to say that . . . ?" "When I read this paragraph/section/proposal, I come away thinking. . . . Is that what you want me to think?" "When I read this section, I have a certain image in my mind about your informants. Is this the image you want me to have?" And then you get to respond: "Yes, that's exactly what I want you to think." or "No, I was not interested in making that point at all. Rather, I wanted to. . . . Tell me, how can I get to where I want to be? What should I change?" This kind of talk is not only extremely helpful for preparing drafts, but it also promotes the kind of discussion about your work that improves the quality of the writing. Your group offers feedback about how what you have said, at least as this audience interprets it, compares to what you wanted to say. You move out of the framework of thinking about your work as either good or bad (not a very useful binary way to frame it) and into a mode of imagining how to use words, phrasing, theory, organization, and style to get it to come out one way rather than another way.

3. A group will give you more energy to complete your project. Group members both give you and your work attention and position you to read closely the work of others and give them attention. If you are anxious about getting attention because you feel it puts you in an unwelcome spotlight, then you will have time to adjust to receiving attention and grow accustomed to this important process. If you enjoy attention and feel that you rarely receive enough, then you will enjoy how the attention accrues. The dialogue that results from close readings of texts will also give you energy because it will stimulate you to think carefully and deeply about your own work and that of others. A writing group should also give you energy because it provides yet another structure to position you close to your writing, your ideas, your intentions, and your argument.

4. Most likely, you will be in a writing group with students who are doing dissertations in fields other than your own. Therefore, they bring to your texts very different understandings than you have about the world, they take for granted things that you do not, and they know less about your field. This means that you cannot get away with referring to concepts that you have not explained. This cross section of people should therefore encourage you to communicate in better ways with your readers.

5. When you are frustrated with your writing, struggling unsuccess-
   fully to say what you want to say, a writing group can help. If you
   have developed trust, you should feel comfortable sharing with the
   group the section you cannot construct the way you want to. Your
   writing group, which should know your work pretty well, can provide a diagnosis.

We have described how a good writing group looks. If you find yourself in a group where some of you work more consistently than others, or
where you always respond to the work of others but are never or rarely
responded to, then you need to decide if the group is worth the time you
devote to it. A dissertation writing group is important if it provides you
support, critique, and alternative ways to consider your work. If the group
does not provide that, you might reconsider your participation.

GETTING STARTED, KEEPING GOING, AND GETTING IT DONE

It is easiest if you are working on the dissertation full time, as if it were a
job, but this is often not the case. Students have jobs, assistantships, and
life. You may be trying to get pregnant, or have a baby, or be worried about
the health of a child or partner or parent. All the complications of life are
poised to intrude. When you begin the full-time writing on the dissertation (and we use *full-time* advisedly, since you will be writing small sections, perhaps in the form of memos, as you go along), it makes a significant
difference if you can have some months to work only on your writing. If
you were not able to work full time on the dissertation while you wrote
the proposal and collected data, apply for a fellowship that would enable
you to write full time for a few months, if it's possible. If not, you will have
to develop a schedule that you can meet.

You are ready to go. You sit down, fingers poised above the keyboard.
How do you actually get started? As we said in an earlier chapter, you
should start with the data chapters. If organizing or planning an entire
chapter seems overwhelming, you can get started by writing memos about
your work. In these memos you might take one of the themes or a particular issue that you want the chapter to discuss and write about it, stating your findings and illustrating them with the data. When you write
several of these, you then have some written work to examine as you
attempt to connect these analyses. Jeff Mangram decided that for his study
of the popular culture interests of social studies teachers he would pre-

pare profiles of two of the teachers he wanted to showcase in his dissertation in order to "get some momentum" in his writing. He wrote these profiles, set them aside, and then, months later, decided that he would shape one of his data chapters around these profiles, expanding from their situations through comparison and contrast to other teachers in his study. Writing the profiles enabled him to make a serious start on a data chapter, but they also served an important purpose in structuring a chapter later, even though he did not know when he was writing them that they would play this role.

If you have written memos about your data during fieldwork and data analysis, you might gather them together to see what sort of forays into writing you have already made. Are there ways that you can link together any of these memos to provide a loosely framed chapter?

What kind of writer do you want to be? What sort of style do you want to use? We often forget that our style of writing reflects choices we make about putting words on paper. There are two kinds of books to read in order to increase your control over your writing. One sort addresses writing itself. Books we have found helpful include *Writing for Social Scientists* (Becker, 1986), filled with practical advice for students in the social sciences; *The Elements of Style* (Strunk & White, 2000) for the basics about sentence construction, word choice, and grammar; *On Writing* (King, 2002), which, though it is a book about how to write fiction, inspires thoughtfulness about any kind of writing; and *Poison Penmanship* (Mitford, 1979), a readable and entertaining book about muckraking writing that offers surprisingly good advice about how to be an effective narrator. While you may not take the particular advice these writers offer, they will make you think about your own tastes and, if you take being a stylist seriously, will enable you to have more choice.

The second sort of book that is useful to read while you write is a good book that you admire even if it is not about your specific topic. Reading social scientists who write well—or, rather, who write in ways you like or respect—stimulates you to write better, to think broadly about how authors approach their topics, and to pick up strategies that might be useful to you. If you have not collected a pile of books that you want to read, ask friends and professors for recommendations of books they have valued. While reading may sometimes be a strategy for postponing writing, it is also a vehicle for expanding your control as a writer. As you examine other authors' judgments/decisions about organizing chapters, the foregrounding of informants or themes, the depth of communication about the research process, and other key issues, you ask yourself what effect you want your work to have on readers.

PERSEVERANCE

Sticking with a dissertation cannot be reduced to having a good schedule and style of writing. Perseverance helps you to stay with a schedule, to follow through even during busy times of your life, and to stay with a project even as doubts grow about it. In the process of writing a dissertation, there will often be a time when you feel that what you are doing is not measuring up to anything. Sometimes this is because you are so close to the topic that you can no longer see how distinctive and good it is. Sometimes this is because you are at a point when data are slow in coming and your research methods might need a tweaking or new strategy. There are no hard-and-fast rules for getting through such periods except to persevere. Often things turn around and, when you least expect it, you may find yourself excited and inspired by the very same project that depressed you a week ago. One doctoral student had good advice for those who end up in such slumps. She wrote about the doubts and slumps in memos and as sections of her fieldnotes. She felt that speaking (or writing) forthrightly about her doubts about and dislike for her project helped her to take control of her feelings by voicing them. She stated in a section of what she called her "self-pitying fieldnotes":

> Today was the fourth meeting of the new schoolyear. I have been attending *Feed Your Mind* sporadically for almost a year now—a few meetings last fall and most weeks last spring. My data are growing. But I am feeling a little overwhelmed, or confused about this project right now. On the one hand, this seems like the most amazing space to learn about kids and what they think about the world. It seems like the perfect place to see gender work, to see language have really significant meaning and to see the struggles over growing up. It seems like a perfect place to see what matters to kids. But I just keep feeling like I "have nothing good" in my notes. I keep writing everything down, typing it in, writing memos to myself, and yet I have no idea how to make sense of my notes. And I have no idea how to get in with these kids in more intimate ways. I keep reading all these ethnographies about youth, and I see the researchers really making connections, and I just don't see that happening here. So then I ask myself, why am I doing this? I hate getting up early. I am not a morning person. Being there at 6:50 really throws off my whole day, when it comes down to it. And if it feels this way, why don't I choose another project? I guess I am just feeling discouraged because I just remember [my advisor] saying, if you hate professional wrestling, don't choose it as your topic. So why have I chosen a topic that I feel

like I have to suffer for? In a few weeks I will need to reassess this and see if this is just a bad mood! (fieldnotes, 10/14/98)

This doctoral student realized that what she called "methodological crises" were as much a part of the project as the data she collected. By looking at other literature and qualitative studies, she discovered that self-doubts and even tears can be a part of any project. She was not alone in her self-doubts but marveled that so little was actually said about "the methodological and conceptual troubles" of writing ethnography. Quite a bit has been written about issues related to methods, representations, and relationships between researchers and informants, but issues about the self-struggle that goes on in the process as you love and then hate your topic and persevere through bad moods, early mornings, and, in the case of one doctoral student, long commutes from rural Australia into the city, or, in the case of another, multiple obligations as the mother of several children, can make it seem like you are the only one going through it. You're not.

Perseverance can sometimes be more than a personal struggle; it can be a struggle with impersonal authorities. Two examples can highlight this point. In one case, a doctoral student, who was studying sexuality at a school where she was employed, was asked to discontinue her dissertation. She was threatened, a grievance was filed against her, and she was evaluated poorly during her tenure review—all because she insisted that she had the right to write about the school and the students. She had the support of her union and most of the parents in the school. Perseverance was for her a matter of remaining calm, as well as taking copious notes of all meetings with the principal (who opposed her) and judicial hearings. She went through all the proper channels, never flew off the handle, and studied her rights. In the end, she gained the support of the school board and all other necessary people to write her dissertation.

In another case, a doctoral student studying the juvenile court system in Philadelphia was asked not to attend court proceedings. The proceedings were open to the public, and his research involved observations of the proceedings. He was told by a judge, orally and in a formal letter, that the court was not a place for conducting research. In response to the judge and in an equally formal letter to the court, he insisted that he was permitted to sit in on the proceedings because they were open to the public. He said that his first reaction when he was approached by the judge was to obey. He claimed that he had collected quite a bit of data already and that the observations of proceedings were actually a small part of the larger dissertation. But his advisor urged him to at least respond and to state that he did have a right to attend the proceedings, which he did. He waited until he was sure that his letter had been received, and then returned to the court to continue his observations. Though he received several cold stares, he was not asked again to leave.

Support to persevere through the research and writing of your dissertation can come from many corners: It may come from partners, advisors, writing or dissertation support groups, fellow graduate students, even from emulating other writers. In other cases, when you must persevere through problems that are more political than personal, it may be important to know your rights and to be sure that you have approval to conduct the research from all necessary individuals. If you are asked to discontinue your research or to not conduct it at all, you may need to know whether you do, in fact, have the right to conduct the research; if you do, get ready for what could be a lengthy and difficult process.

WRITING AS STYLE

People have their own styles of writing—not only a linguistic style but also a style of approaching the work of writing. Writing a dissertation takes style, and sometimes this entails a lifestyle change. For the person who enjoys leisurely early mornings, or sleeping in, an alarm clock and a new way of passing the mornings might be needed. A common assertion among doctoral students is that you need to find the time to write. Finding the time depends on you. Some people can't function in the evenings, some have children, some have jobs, and we all have other obligations. So establishing a schedule (even a flexible schedule) and sticking to it is clearly an important part of writing. As one doctoral student rapped, "Pages don't get written unless you're sittin'." A spattering of lessons can be gleaned from comments by dissertation writers. They included one anthropology graduate student who said that taking a walk in the morning, pouring a cup of coffee, cleaning her eyeglasses, and turning on the computer were all part of a routine that got her ready for writing (see Becker, 1986, for helpful discussions of these rituals). Another doctoral student explained:

> I used other writers as examples. I'm not talking about people writing dissertations, but novelists. People like Virginia Woolf, Balzac, who were almost maniacal about writing. They made it seem romantic, writing against all odds, writing through the night, being obsessed about it. I wasn't like that, but I said to myself unless I am going to be a writer, I'm not going to get this thing written.

Another doctoral student worked full time and needed to leave early in the morning, but she was usually home from work by 4:00. Her child was in day care until about 5:00.

> A single mother working part time is about as hard as it can get for writing a dissertation. But I do it with a routine. One hour in the afternoon, every afternoon, even if I don't do much writing, I sit at my stool with my computer at the counter, and work. Then, after my son goes to bed, I do another hour. I don't shut off my computer between that time, so I know I have to shut off my computer after my son goes to bed, so I go over feeling like I have no energy, but then I reread what I did in the [afternoon], and usually I'll make some changes, add a section, or do some task, and I end up working for another hour or so. I always tell myself I'll write until I finish my cup of tea.

Some people are overwhelmed with obligations, while others, especially those who receive funding to complete their dissertations, might find themselves without "a good-enough schedule."

> My problem was too much time on my hands without a good-enough schedule. When I was in graduate school, I was a research assistant in another department. I worked 20 hours each week, took full-time classes, then worked in the evenings on my papers. Now, I am taking a year off to write and I feel like I don't have the schedule to get me actually writing. I do a lot of reading, I tell myself to get ready to write, but then I go online, I tell myself to get some information for my writing, but in the end I'm not really writing. This is what I call procrastination.

The doctoral student decided that he would not permit himself to play guitar (this was his first love) until he had written at least two pages of his dissertation.

Another dissertation writer prepared a weekly schedule for her work:

> I told myself that I needed to write for at least 15 hours each week, you know, about 2 to 3 hours each day with a little weekend work thrown in there. I have a reading group that is actually a bunch of people from a class we took together, and we e-mail each other to check up on each of us and meet once a week. You know, they'll ask me how much I wrote and I'll make sure that they did, too.

Another doctoral student took a lesson from her kids. "When my kids were little, we'd hang a calendar on the refrigerator and check off things like that they did their homework or they cleaned their room. We'd make them check it off, whatever it was." She used the same strategy for herself, checking off each day the number of pages she wrote. She had a goal for each Friday and stuck to it for the most part. Everybody has his or her own style, and finding your style of writing is much like finding your voice.

USING YOUR TIME

In writing a dissertation, it is helpful to prepare a schedule for completing specific chapters. Timetables are an effective way to move the dissertation along because they provide goals that you try and reach. Even if you cannot meet each target date, the presence of the date offers a frame for analyzing your progress. You can then see whether you are on target, a week or two behind, or really off schedule. If you are really off schedule, you may have devised a timetable that is unrealistic or unworkable for you. And remember, you construct a timetable to help you manage the writing, not to make yourself guilt-ridden or overly self-critical. But having a schedule is important because you need several months after finishing a real draft before you can bring it to defense. Given the need for multiple drafts that respond to commentary from your advisor and from committee members, an April defense date, for example, demands that the first full draft that you give your advisor be completed sometime in January. When doctoral students come to us somewhere near the beginning of the writing process asking how to figure out whether they can defend in April (or September or June), we take out a piece of paper and write an April or September or June date at the top of it and then work back, accounting for the weeks when advisors are reading the dissertation before offering comments, time for your rewrites, time for other committee members to read it, and the time that our college requires that readers have the document before the defense (different universities have specific policies on when the committee needs the final draft before the defense, but universities usually require 2 to 3 weeks). Students are usually surprised at the length of time it takes. A timetable helps you to figure in the weeks that count in this process when the document is out of your hands.

Even with a timetable, good intentions, and self-discipline, there will be times when you find yourself making little progress—you cannot concentrate; you lose your focus; you are not sure what you want to write. Whatever the reason, this sometimes happens. Rather than stop all work, undertake another of the many tasks involved in producing a dissertation.

Work on the reference list, get citations for quotations you have used, read a few articles for your literature review, or look for data examples to illustrate your themes. Different tasks demand varied levels of concentration; some tasks take time but are less challenging than others. Keep a running list of things that need to be done. Sometimes, rewriting or editing sections will help you to work through the frustration, but when you are unsuccessful, turn to another task.

A FEW WORDS ON STYLE

We said that this chapter would focus on the work of writing rather than writing style, but there are two issues we cannot ignore. When we read dissertations, we notice them and usually comment in the margins.

Use the Active Voice Whenever Possible

Many successful writers, including several of the ones we have mentioned in this chapter (e.g., Becker, 1986; Strunk & White, 2002), emphasize the importance of the active voice. You are forced, when you use the active voice, to account for human agency. Writing in the active voice moves the text along. The passive voice allows you to say that things get done to people without saying who has done them; lets you, as the writer, off the hook; and leaves the reader wondering what happened. Since much academic writing in journals depends on the passive voice, models of writing that let us off the hook surround us. To contrast how these narrative voices appear to the reader, we will use our own work to show our preference for the active voice.

We draw the first example from an article that argues that when adult researchers study young people, their reliance on their own memories may hamper their insight even as it enhances their narrative authority. The first sentence of the article moves the article along:

> Like it or not, ethnographers who study youth often travel down memory lane to revisit their own adolescence. . . . More common than uncommon, these references reaffirm an adult's status as a former youth. With such a status, narrators announce that they are not complete strangers to their informants. Rather, these narrators bring some experience to bear on their projects that increases their interpretive authority. (Biklen, 2004, p. 715)

The active voice contributes to the pace.

Later in the article, however, the author reverts to the passive voice: "People are born within particular political climates, climates that can shape the shared values of many in a generation. When generations talk to each other, there are barriers that must be crossed to communicate" (Biklen, 2004, p. 721). The construction of this section is much weaker. The last sentence should read, "When generations talk to each other, they must cross barriers to communicate." This revised sentence is not only grammatically correct, but it does not let the author off of the hook. It says who must do the border crossing (both generations), while the previous version of the sentence suggests that perhaps only the adults have barriers to cross. The active voice forces writers to be more specific.

In the second example, we show the use of the passive voice from a book about gender and teaching. "First, careers take place in the public sphere and are measured by an individual's participation in the wage-labor system and by the status that accrues from that participation" (Biklen, 1995, p. 24). In this discussion of the social construction of "career," the use of the passive voice ("careers . . . are measured by") means that the author does not have to articulate who is doing the measuring. Does she refer to sociologists who study careers with methods and models? Is it citizens who are observers of teachers' lives? The passive voice weakens the sentence because it freed us from saying, as we should have, who we meant.

The third example comes from a book that examines how companies market security technology for schools:

> During the last several years of studying violence and security in schools, I have seen school authorities in a variety of districts enter into deals with security businesses to purchase metal detectors, keypad locks on all classroom doors, surveillance cameras with pan-tilt-zoom capabilities, shoulder microphones for school police, and handheld mobile computers that are used, in part, to keep track of students in hallways. (Casella, 2006, p. 2)

The active voice that dominates the first part of the sentence, together with the rich detail of different technological devices, leaves no question that school leaders want these devices. At the end of the sentence, when we switch into the passive voice ("computers that are used"), we don't communicate clearly to the reader who is actually keeping track of the students. Is it police officers? Teachers? Staff? The active voice would have forced us to articulate who actually used the equipment. A few passive constructions will slip into any academic writing, but you should avoid it as much as you can.

Avoid the Ethnographic Present

When we write up qualitative and ethnographic research, we may feel like we have a choice about whether to write in the past or present tense. The danger of writing the narrative in the present tense is the effect of stasis.

When you study a setting, a group of informants, or a theme across settings, you study something that changes over time. People may behave as they did when you observed them but may not behave that way 3 or 5 or 10 years later. When you write in the present tense, you suggest that the slice of life you studied will always remain the way it was when you were there. When you use the past tense, however, you suggest that time makes a difference.

In a chapter about how two towns that he studied have changed over the years, anthropologist Clifford Geertz (1995) emphasized how deep the changes have been.

> The problem is that more has changed, and more disjointly, than one at first imagines. The two towns of course have altered, in many ways superficially, in a few profoundly. But so, and likewise, has the anthropologist. So has the discipline within which the anthropologist works, the intellectual setting within which that discipline exists, and the moral basis on which it rests. So have the countries in which the two towns are enclosed and the international world in which the two countries are enclosed. So has just about everyone's sense of what is available from a life. (pp. 1–2)

While using the past tense when writing up a study does not entail the complications that Geertz so richly describes, it gestures to them. You do not want to give the impression that when you were there, you captured the world you studied as it was and still is. Let others reaffirm the continuity and significance of your work (see also Davis, 1992).

One of the confusions that this advice sometimes generates relates to the relationship between the writing of fieldnotes and the dissertation narrative. You may write your fieldnotes in the present tense:

> As I walk into the room, I notice that all of the nurses who are on break are sitting around a small table, laughing at a newspaper article that Bettina is reading to them. (June 4, 1999)

> "Do you want any of this great lasagna that one of the patient's parents brought for us?" Jill asks me as I walk in. Jill, Bettina, Mary, and Nellie are eating lasagna from paper plates. It smells great, so I say, "Sure, if you have enough." (October 8, 2000)

If you use these fieldnote excerpts in a chapter, you would keep the examples in the present tense, just as you wrote them in the field, but narrate the story in the past tense. You might write something like: "The nurses at Blixon Hospital frequently used the Billington Family room to socialize with each other." Then you would illustrate that claim with the two fieldnote excerpts above. If you do not write your fieldnotes in the present tense, you may find it less confusing.

Since we frequently use participant observation fieldnotes as part of the narrative in qualitative data chapters, we would have to translate our fieldnotes in that case. We might transform our fieldnotes, in that case, from data to narrative. Here is an example of what that might look like in this fictional case:

> The nurses at Blixon Hospital frequently used the Billington Family room to socialize with each other. On several occasions when I hung out there during the afternoon, I observed their friendly interactions. One afternoon, for example, I observed all of the nurses who were on break sitting around a small table sharing laughter over a newspaper article that Bettina read out loud. On another occasion a group of four nurses sat together, eating hot lasagna that one of the patient's parents had brought in. While life was not always this relaxed, I saw these exchanges on enough occasions to realize their importance.

There are many ways of using data in your narrative, but however you do, try to communicate to your reader that your informants are not imprisoned by your foray into their world.

CHAPTER 8

The Defense of the Qualitative Dissertation

The dissertation defense is not the same thing to all the people who are there. As a qualitative researcher, you understand the social construction of reality, the idea of "the definition of the situation" (Thomas, 1923). That is, situations do not have intrinsic meaning but rather carry meanings attributed to them. In specific situations, people act on the basis of their interpretation, or "definition," of the situation. As the "candidate" of the moment, however, you might not be thinking like a qualitative researcher. You might be feeling instead like a person on "the hot seat."

You might be feeling many things at once: pride in your work that will now be officially recognized; that you are at a key point in a "rite of passage" that will move you from the student role to the professional role; a bit defensive as you foresee (or worse, imagine) the kinds of questions that you will be asked; and happiness that it's almost over. At different moments in the few weeks before your defense, some of these feelings may surge into the foreground for a few days and then fade into the background, while others are simultaneously doing the opposite.

Dissertation advisors hold multiple feelings as well. They may be happy for you at the end of this journey for the doctorate; wondering how you will respond to the questions the examining committee will put to you; looking forward to your performance at the event; and, like all faculty members at these occurrences, hoping for a stimulating intellectual discussion.

Remember that, for you, this is a once in a lifetime event. Professors, on the other hand, attend many of these defenses year after year. While your advisor may be deeply invested in the intellectual contribution you are making to a field, other faculty prefer to have a stimulating discussion rather than a boring few hours where the candidate answers the questions well but fails to generate a spark. Of course, this is a bit of an exaggeration. Faculty members want to be connected to competence and to see you perform well. But you may interpret a lively discussion as an attack or as skepticism, while the faculty members are stimulated and happy to have interesting questions generated about the document.

The above discussion has put forth several issues that we want to examine in this chapter: These include a description of the occasion, preparation for the defense, the defense as a performance, and anxiety. We begin with a definition of the defense.

THE DEFENSE: A DEFINITION AND DESCRIPTION

After you have completed a written draft of your dissertation—and this does not mean a first draft—you seek approval from your dissertation chair or from your core committee, depending on your university's policies, to bring the dissertation to a defense. While schools have different policies about the state of a draft, most universities share varieties of forms of "passing" your defense. These categories usually include some version of the following sorts of evaluations: pass, pass with distinction, pass with minor revisions to be supervised by the advisor, pass with major revisions that the whole committee must approve, and fail. A defense is an occasion where your committee and readers meet to hear you respond to questions about the document that you have worked to produce. The defense is chaired by a university representative from the graduate school who is there to ensure that the defense is conducted in an impartial manner and to act as a kind of master/mistress of ceremonies, ensuring that procedures are followed, that all committee members have a chance to ask questions if they should or if they desire to, and to make sure that all of the forms are signed and turned in. Most universities have open defenses where friends, guests, and people interested in the topic or in learning about a dissertation defense may attend. They may not attend all parts of the defense, however. When committee members and the candidate are in the room, universities usually have a policy of asking the candidate and all guests to leave for a few minutes so that procedures can be worked out. If faculty members from different colleges at a university are on the committee, for example, the defense chair and the committee members need to share an understanding of how the event will flow. Who will ask the first questions? How will the rotation of questioners proceed? These are some of the issues that the committee will discuss while you are out of the room.

Sometimes the committee will also discuss the candidate and the dissertation. A defense chair might ask, "Does anyone have any problems with the defense proceeding?" or "Does anyone have serious questions about this study?" If you have a good dissertation chair and communicate well with this person, you should not be in a defense where a member of the examining committee can respond, "Yes, I have serious problems with this dissertation, and I don't think the defense should proceed." Your dissertation advisor should be clear that your work is strong enough for the defense to proceed, and if he or she does not think that it is ready, you should not be defending. Some schools have created a structure to lessen the chance that a dissertation will go to defense where the faculty do not support it. At the School of Education at Syracuse University, for example, in addition to a core committee of three faculty, two "outside readers"—that is, faculty who are not members of your department—are given the dissertation 3 weeks before the defense date, after they have agreed to be readers. Forty-eight hours before the defense, they must turn in "readers' comments" about the dissertation. In addition to containing a space for the reader's commentary and questions, the form contains three questions:

1. Should the oral defense of this dissertation proceed as planned?
   _____ yes _____ no
2. Acceptability of dissertation:
   _____ Acceptable in its present form
   _____ Acceptable with *minor* revisions as noted
   _____ Acceptable with *major* revisions as noted
3. Summary of concerns:
   _____ a) Form and style
   _____ b) Basic design
   _____ c) Data collection
   _____ d) Data analysis
   _____ e) Review of related theory and research
   _____ f) Other(s): _____

While the readers' comments and questions are the most important issue for the defense, the dissertation advisor and the candidate need to have a response from readers that the defense should proceed. Again, a good advisor (and a good doctoral student) should not be wondering 48 hours before the scheduled defense if it should proceed. But if this happens, and it has, this reader's form can prevent a group meeting where the outcome will be doomed.

The defense itself, usually scheduled as about a 2-hour session, opens with the candidate making a presentation about the dissertation. Specific amounts of time are allotted for this presentation; at universities across the country the times range from 10 to 20 minutes. Your university will have its own guidelines for these presentations, but there are many strategies to consider for your talk. Each strategy has strengths and weaknesses, so you should consider the examining committee, the perspectives of committee members and readers on your work, and the expectations for this presentation in your environment.

One strategy is to summarize your key findings and emphasize both the contribution to the literature and the significance of your work. Students who choose this strategy often employ a PowerPoint presentation. The strength of this form of presentation is that it provides you with an opportunity to emphasize clearly for the entire committee your major points and the emphasis you believe these points deserve. A weakness of this strategy is that committee members have recently read or reread your dissertation, and such a presentation can sound a bit like something they have already heard and know too well.

A second strategy incorporates in the presentation responses to the criticisms that committee members have raised about your dissertation. Obviously, this strategy only works if you know some of these critiques in advance. In this approach, you talk about your dissertation and address some of the comments about your work. You may still have to answer questions later, but you can show how, from your perspective, your work addresses the concerns that readers might have. For one student's defense, a reader had commented that the researcher had not written about how well she came to know her informants. In the opening presentation, the candidate addressed part of her statement to this issue without ever saying directly that she was responding to the comment. One strength of this approach is that you initiate commentary about the topic rather than defensively responding to a query from a professor about it. A weakness is that the committee member's concern may have been relatively minor, and if you spend too much time addressing it in your opening remarks, you give it too much importance.

Still another strategy might emphasize the methodology of the dissertation. This approach emphasizes the content less than questions of design, fieldwork, analysis, depending on what the more interesting and significant issues were that arose in your work. You would choose this form of presentation if the methodological issues form one of the important contributions of your work or if you had an especially difficult or interesting time in the field. If you used methods that are not commonly used at your school, this might be a good approach. Faculty might be especially interested in hearing about your work with multisite ethnography if they are unfamiliar with it. They might want to know what it means to employ feminist methodology when your dissertation does not focus particularly on women or gender.

The opening presentation centers the attention of the examining committee on you as a presenter and as an intellectual. Clearly, you may combine any of the strategies suggested above, as long as you base your decision on an analysis of the event. Usually you would discuss your presentation with your faculty advisor in advance. In the opening presentation you have an opportunity to set a tone for the discussion, to try to influence the agenda of the discussion.

At the end of this opening presentation, the floor opens to questions. Traditions about who asks the first question vary at different universities. At some schools, the advisor asks the first question, an honorary role that publicly acknowledges the advisor's work. At other universities, those committee members who have been least involved in the development of the dissertation ask the first questions. These might be readers who have just read the dissertation and written readers' comments or the committee members who have been least involved. Faculty take turns asking the candidate questions, and they may have a dialogue among themselves on certain issues if they are particularly invested in them or if there is some strong disagreement. Sometimes faculty may jump into a dialogue between the candidate and another professor if they think they can clarify a misunderstanding.

At one dissertation defense, one faculty member was isolated by the other committee members because he was the only person who took a particular view on the dissertation. The committee member thought that the dissertation "trashed teachers," while none of the other committee members had this reaction. During the discussion between this committee member and the candidate, other faculty spoke up, trying both to understand why the lone committee member had such a reaction and offering their contrasting comments. The dissertation was passed with distinction and later won an award, but it was a lively discussion while the examining committee members were all in the same room. Though the professor was critical of the student's work, the student did not have to bear all of the weight of handling his concerns, as the other committee members also played a role.

At the end of the period of questioning, the candidate (and all outside guests) will be asked to leave the room while the committee votes and decides whether the dissertation passes, or what form of pass will be granted and what revisions will be required. Then the candidate comes back in for the congratulations.

PREPARATION FOR THE DEFENSE

In Finland, many people undertake Nordic walking as a form of exercise. Nordic walking involves walking with two walking sticks, one in each hand. These sticks look a lot like ski poles, only they have little rubber feet on the bottom tips rather than metal points, they are missing the bottom ring, and they are adjustable in height. To do Nordic walking, the walker simply walks along using the poles, planting each one as a step is taken. The exercise thus involves the arms as well as the legs. When we were working in Finland a few years ago and noticed these poles for the first time, we were interested in them as a form of exercise. On a more recent trip, we noticed much more about how they were used. Our greater familiarity with these Nordic poles and this way of exercising enabled us to be more sophisticated observers. We now noticed that the walkers did not pump their arms as they planted the poles in front of their feet at each step, but rather slanted the poles so that they did not have to raise their arms so high with each step. It was our familiarity with this form of exercise that enabled us to see it in a more detailed way.

Use this metaphor with the dissertation defense. The more you attend as a spectator, the more familiar you will be with how defenses work. You will be able to see variations in defenses and learn more about the range of ways in which committee members might behave.

In addition to reading through your dissertation several times, another important preparation for the defense is to read some good books related to your study but not specifically part of your literature review. You want to look at how researchers approach their topic and prepare for the larger questions about meanings and implications that examining committee members might ask.

THE DEFENSE AS A PERFORMANCE

If you write an excellent dissertation but stumble through your defense, struggling to articulate your responses to questions, you will not fail the defense. If you write a borderline dissertation but perform excellently at the defense, showing your familiarity with the material, your insight into the data, and a command of the issues your dissertation raises, your committee may leave the room more satisfied with your work than when they entered. If your dissertation is competent or of average quality, a stellar defense might make your committee think that you should pass with distinction. If your dissertation is of poor quality, even a great performance at the defense will not get you out of trouble.

When we speak of the defense as a performance, we refer to the idea that the defense of the dissertation occurs in a public arena, where you display your understanding of the work you have done and of its implications as if you were on a stage. You are not an actor, but you are in the role of "the candidate."

When committee members come to a defense, they have expectations of how a candidate will behave. When you meet their expectations by speaking of your work in a knowledgeable manner or by considering in an open-minded way the questions that the committee asks, you satisfactorily perform the role of candidate. Performance, then, refers to the expectations committee members have of what kind of talk demonstrates knowledge of your research and the wider issues your work raises. The fact is that this talk occurs in a public space where professors (and others) watch you as you discuss your work and respond to questions, and you should not comport yourself at a defense in the same way you would in other situations.

Professors do not expect that there is a single way to perform as candidate at a defense. Nor do they enact their performances as examining committee members in light of a single criterion. Students can be nervous, confident, expansive, restrained, humorous, or uptight—and still give the kind of performance that the examining committee expects. One feature of the performance demands particular attention and will serve you well in a defense: openness.

Open-Minded Stance

To be open-minded at a defense, you need to listen closely to the questions committee members ask you and work to understand what their concerns are. When different people read your dissertation, they bring their interests and knowledge to the text, and their questions reflect their reading of your words. They may have particular interests that are more significant to them than they are to you. If your dissertation takes a sociological approach to the topic but one of the examining committee members does history, her questions may center on the historical implications of the topic. Or a reader may wonder why your discussion of the relationship between agency and social structure centered on the work of Anthony Giddens with no mention of Pierre Bourdieu's important scholarship. Your stance must be that you see these as good questions. While your dissertation cannot be all things to all people, the questions that professors ask often cause you to think about the effects of your work differently.

Earlier in the book we described a situation in which one faculty member's response to a dissertation draft was that it was not theoretical enough but another professor wanted more description. While neither committee member demanded that the student meet his or her expectations in preparing a draft of the dissertation for the defense, they both used the occasion of the defense to ask questions about their interests. The defense was lively and stimulating to the faculty who were there. Their questions promoted a discussion that perfectly illustrated the relationship between theory and data that Bourdieu and Wacquant (1992) describe so well: "Every act of research is simultaneously empirical (it confronts the world of observable phenomena) and theoretical (it necessarily engages hypotheses) about the underlying structure of relations that observations are designed to capture" (p. 35). The candidate was not expected to tailor her work to the particular interests of the examining committee members, but she did have to understand the importance of their questions, be able to describe why she negotiated the data–theory connection as she did, and understand how her dissertation might be seen by a wide range of readers bringing multiple interests to the reading.

In the above example, perhaps we have emphasized a bit too much that being open-minded simply means understanding the perspective of a committee member who asks a difficult question. Committee members often raise questions that you ought to have addressed in your dissertation. In this case, you need to respond by showing either how your dissertation does indeed address the question, perhaps in a different form than the committee member saw or wanted, or how you could address it.

An open-minded stance also demonstrates that your dissertation, if competently done, is a starting place for discussion rather than the endpoint. Faculty may ask questions that your dissertation has stimulated them to think about. Responses to these questions may not be contained within the borders of your dissertation. But you perform well when you are able to understand the implications of your work as well as its specific contributions. If your dissertation addresses the inclusion experiences of children with physical disabilities, and a professor asks about any connections you might make to children with intellectual disabilities, your response should not be, "That was not the topic I studied." A response might start out something like: "That is an important question, and I'm glad you raised it. I want to study it in my next project by following a group of kids with intellectual disabilities from preschool through second grade. But I have been thinking that the kinds of barriers each group faces must be different." The questioner did not expect you to have studied his interest but wanted to see how expansive you could be on your interests.

Or if your dissertation is on the perspectives of social studies teachers on popular culture, and a committee member asks how their perspectives differ from those of English teachers or science teachers, you want to interpret the question as one of interest rather than as an attack on your work. Questioners know that you do not know how other teachers in the specific schools you studied think about popular culture, but you might be familiar with some literature on the questions. Part of the performance is showing the respect you have for the question.

Open-mindedness is particularly important when political and ideological differences arise. Being open-minded does not mean that you compromise your stance or position on the issues. It does mean that you hear the assumptions the questioner has about how the world is structured. When particular issues are "hot" and the committee represents a range of views, rearticulating your approach while acknowledging that you understand the perspectives of the questioner is an important strategy. Let's assume your work is about "decolonizing methodologies" (Smith, 1999), for example, and you have made an effort in your work on indigenous people to resist what you have defined as colonizing research approaches. If you can articulate the principles of this approach and describe the models for your work without sounding defensive when a faculty member raises a question about whether or not your approach is "scientific," this means that you can describe your position without sounding defensive. In the example discussed above, where the faculty member told a student she had "trashed teachers," taking this stance meant that the faculty member rather than the student became defensive.

The doctoral defense is a rite of passage of sorts that most candidates worry about. When we describe it as a performance, we do not mean that it is "fake" rather than "real." We mean that everyone enters the defense with a set of expectations. Since the examining committee has more authority than the candidate, it is helpful for the student to be able to perform the role well and meet the expectations that you will know your work and be open to the questions of committee members.

Anxiety

When you arrive at your defense, you are anxious. Even if you felt confident about the quality of your work when you turned in the draft a few weeks ago, at the moment of the defense you feel as if you are on stage and perhaps not certain about your abilities as a performer. Anxiety on the part of candidates is so normal that when candidates tell us they are anxious, we often say, "That's all right. A little anxiety is part of the process." Notice that we used the adjective *little*.

So much more rides on the dissertation itself than on the defense, but you research and write the dissertation over a period of months or years and defend it in a couple of hours. The brief time period of the defense compresses energy and raises anxiety. The most important part of the defense is the work you have done. If you and your advisor are confident that your dissertation draft is ready to defend, then you want to do the work you need to do to imagine the dissertation defense as a stimulating 2 hours that will challenge, energize, and teach you.

It is easy to redirect the anxiety toward worry about how readers not involved with earlier drafts will respond to your work. One student wondered whether two faculty she knew well could be readers for the dissertation. The chair recognized this kind of query for the anxiety it represented and responded, "Neither of them can be a reader, [name omitted]. And stop worrying—you wrote a great dissertation!!!!!!!!!!!!!!!!!!!!!!!!!!!!!!!!!!!!!!! Get my point?"

The anxiety before a dissertation defense comes from feeling that the situation is out of your control. And if you feel this, you are partly right. You are right because you cannot predict what will happen at the event. You do not know whether the faculty sitting around the table will "like" your work. While you want the admiration of faculty whom you admire, you should remember that the examining committee does not have to "like" or be particularly interested in your work in order to pass it. They only have to think it is competent.

Your anxiety has probably been lowered if you have prepared for your defense by attending other defenses in your department or college. You then have some experience to draw on to imagine what your defense will be like.

What you come in prepared to talk about depends on what you know about the examining committee and about your material. If you are particularly worried that some committee members do not understand the qualitative approach, then you want to make sure you are well prepared to talk about methodological aspects of your research. If you are worried that some committee members do not completely understand what it means to do online research, and this was the focus of your project, you want to make sure to have many examples of this burgeoning field of qualitative studies that you can draw on to illustrate your points. You might also talk about how research on online communities has affected methods or procedures among qualitative scholars.

Your dissertation advisor should also help with your anxiety. Not only should you be able to talk through your worries and help plan for a strong defense with your advisor, but you should also know a bit about how the role of the advisor changes at the defense. Up until that moment, the role of the advisor is to push, stimulate, challenge, and support you to write the best dissertation you can (and to get it done). At the defense, the advisor's role shifts a bit. It now moves to a more protectionist role (that is, if the advisor is confident in your work) to contain the number of revisions that might be asked of you. The advisor does not want to inhibit committee members from asking for revisions. Often revisions cover concerns that the dissertation did not address and should have. Rather, the advisor works to make sure that the revisions asked of you are necessary, not just reflective of a committee member's particular interest.

While you may be sick of the dissertation by the time you get to the defense, your goal should always be to write an important work on a topic you care deeply about. When we hear students say that they just have to get it done and want to do a "quick-and-dirty project," we take such comments with a grain of salt. You should care about your work. Many students who thought they were doing controversial or cutting-edge dissertations and worried about faculty response to them had nothing to fear from the defense because they had worked hard, had an open stance in the defense, and knew their material. It is so important not to let fear of faculty responses inhibit you from taking intellectual risks with your work. As long as you have a dissertation chair or committee who supports these risks, or at least who comes to support them, you enter your dissertation defense strongly positioned.

It is important to remember that faculty learn from the defenses in which they participate and from good work that challenges their taken-for-granted approaches—and that they enjoy a good and stimulating discussion. The academy should be a site where all participants continually learn from the work they do and where we learn from one another. On the day of your defense, go in with the idea that you have something to teach while you also defend the choices you made, the ideas you have, and the work you did.

CHAPTER 9

Nontraditional Dissertations

When you write a qualitative dissertation, the context in which you write it—particularly your department's or college's support for qualitative methods, the familiarity of professors with the range of styles that are possible, and the kind of research that a professor or a department is willing to support—encourages particular kinds of dissertations. It is part of your work as a doctoral student, then, to discover the context in which you are writing your dissertation. Here are some examples. In a setting where qualitative dissertations are common, a number of faculty in your area undertake qualitative research themselves, and there is a developed sequence of qualitative methods courses available, qualitative dissertations do not stand out as unusual or noticeable. But in a context where few faculty undertake or support qualitative research, doing a traditional qualitative dissertation may itself be viewed as nontraditional. These contrasting settings promote different environments for doing qualitative dissertations. While there may be leeway for more nontraditional qualitative work in the first setting, this may be resisted in the second.

These contexts, however, are not static. If they were, change would never occur. Qualitative methods expanded because researchers were interested in narrative approaches to data, in the idea of voice, in the question of who got studied and why, and in figuring out the terrain of problems that had not hitherto been addressed, such as studying people labeled intellectually disabled from the perspectives of the subjects themselves. The antiracist movement, feminism, LGBT studies, and social activism, as well as changes in cultural politics, pushed empirical research to account for issues that earlier researchers barely attended to. So when you look at your particular university's context for dissertation research, remember that eventually it can change and that you can play a role in the shift if you so desire.

In all of this, you have to decide what kind of a doctoral student you are. Are you someone who wants to push on these issues to write a particular kind of dissertation because you are passionate about it? Are you someone who would like to write an autoethnography but does not know how to take a group of faculty or even your advisor on? Is there a cohort writing their dissertations at the same time who agree that you would all like to push the limits of what is traditionally allowed? Is there a faculty member in your department or on campus who is known as a nontraditional qualitative researcher, or who is ardent about alternative approaches? Each of these situations provides different clues for you in making your decision about what to do. Finally, there is the big question we must address: Is it a good idea to write a nontraditional dissertation? In this chapter, we lay out how we define a nontraditional dissertation, discuss why people are attracted to these modes of representation, present some of the issues and concerns of such dissertations, and end with some advice.

WHAT IS A NONTRADITIONAL DISSERTATION?

There is no single example of the nontraditional dissertation since, as we said, what is traditional at one university may be nontraditional at another. In some ways, we could point to newer forms of qualitative methods, such as institutional ethnography (DeVault & McCoy, 2002) or online interviewing (Johns, Chen, & Hall, 2004) as nontraditional. These are approaches that are newer ways of doing qualitative research, and they would probably not be understood as traditional approaches to a qualitative dissertation. They share, however, an empirical grounding with other, more traditional methods. Here, we use *nontraditional dissertations* to refer to dissertations that push the boundaries of dissertation writing through their challenges to methods of empirical research. They do not just employ critical race theory or feminist methods to gather and analyze data, even though they may also use these theoretical frames; they may also employ such methods as fiction writing and personal memoir. In other words, they challenge the distinction between empirical research and fictional work, blurring the boundaries between personal narrative and more traditional qualitative empirical styles (see Goodhall, 2000). They push what social scientists, specifically qualitative social scientists, understand as an empirical frame for the dissertation. They are attracted to particular forms of narrating and representing the data, including autoethnography, film or multi-media, and fictional components.

An example of a nontraditional dissertation is that of J. B. Zuckerman (2001), a dissertation about a progressive urban school that wove fictional ghost stories into the text in order to communicate how the school and its current milieu were haunted by those who were no longer there. This approach also enabled Zuckerman to write about the impact of the school's earlier founders and participants and other issues without violating the confidentiality of her informants, always a concern in the case study of a small setting. This dissertation form, then, addressed two conceptual problems: how to handle particularly sticky confidentiality issues, and how to represent the idea that even though particular figures no longer were materially present on campus, their legacies were prominent.

This dissertation can be called nontraditional because the ghost stories, while based on real events, were not constructed to represent what the researcher saw and heard in the contexts in which the events, issues, and stories were seen and heard. Research that constructs composite characters also veers toward the nontraditional in similar ways. The narrative in the traditional qualitative dissertation works to show how carefully the researcher collected the data so that the reader can make judgments about the quality of the data. While the authors of nontraditional dissertations also have to know their data very well and be particularly good writers to successfully accomplish an innovative approach, the reader of such dissertations is less able to evaluate the data or the relationship between the data and the analysis.

THE ATTRACTIONS OF THE FORM

What attracts researchers to nontraditional forms of presenting qualitative data can probably be summed up by the terms *politics* and *posts*. We are using the word *posts* to refer to postcolonialism and poststructuralism. We employ *politics* to mean movements for social justice, such as antiracist work, feminism, the disability rights movement, and queer theory, all of which are concerned with changing power relations.

Poststructuralism, identity politics, and postpositivism have pushed ethnographic researchers to signify the researcher's own identity in relation to a project's informants. An ethnographer's and informant's shared ethnic, racial, gender, or national identity, for example, has sometimes been represented as improving access and has sometimes been analyzed for the complications posed (see, e.g., De Andrade, 2000; Lather & Smithies, 1997; Nelson, 1996; Villenas, 1996). Research by more powerful researchers on informants who have been constructed as Other raises red flags of objectification or "exoticism" (Gupta & Ferguson, 1997) and the problem of speaking for others (Alcoff, 1991/1992). Poststructuralism's articulation of the impossibility of the "view from nowhere" (Haraway, 1988) had a practical effect on much ethnographic work—the narrator's insertion of personal information to situate the knowledge produced, and to account for the ethnographer's gaze. The researchers themselves, in other words, become part of the narration. While researcher location has become much more standard in the traditional dissertation as well, in the nontraditional dissertation, the boundary between talking about self as a question of method and making self part of the topic of study blurs. In autoethnography, for example, the researcher's self becomes a significant part of the study. The experiences of an author need to be added and cannot be contained within a discussion of subjectivity.

Scholars have been attracted to nontraditional forms because the traditions of qualitative methods seem to have excluded their people or their people's concerns (however they define their people and their people's concerns). These are the political issues related to the nontraditional dissertation. Clair (2003) and others have emphasized the "colonial underpinnings of ethnographic practices" (xi). Qualitative work has a history, or to be more accurate, histories. Researchers are invested in these traditions for different reasons and to different degrees. Those researchers who write for and with a community and do not find this orientation emphasized enough in the tradition will look for other ways to get this view represented in the work.

Beth Ferri, for example, was concerned with how people with disabilities were represented in scholarship. At the same time, she wanted to follow a more feminist approach to qualitative research and undertake collaborative work with her informants. She felt that this mode would be less objectifying of a group of people commonly objectified than if she took a more traditional approach. In her study of women with learning disabilities (Ferri, 1997), she constructed an advisory committee outside of her dissertation committee at the university, consisting of four women with learning disabilities who were also participants in her study. These women helped analyze the data and helped to construct an analysis. Ferri constructed a digest of the data by taking out all identifying information, and then sent it around to all of the members of her advisory committee. Since all of the data had been collected online, the informants' views were not geographically restricted to a single location. While this approach is not the same as writing a partially fictional account of research, it does share with other nontraditional dissertations the idea that the researcher shares the power of analysis with the informants, and hence interrogates the researcher's position.

CONSIDERING THE NONTRADITIONAL
QUALITATIVE DISSERTATION

This chapter began by addressing some concerns about undertaking a non-traditional qualitative dissertation, particularly those related to the energy and persona necessary to complete one. The attractions of this kind of dissertation were highlighted in the previous section. In this section we explore some of the issues to consider if you are attracted to such a dissertation form.

The foremost concern is finding a dissertation advisor who will support your doing such work. While it is not impossible to find such an advisor, it can be difficult, and you will really need the support of your advisor to accomplish such a dissertation. Several dissertation advisors we spoke with said things like, "I don't encourage more experimental types of dissertations, but if a student is really interested and committed to doing this kind of work, I wouldn't stand in the way." Another advisor said, "To write this kind of dissertation, students have to know their data very well and be very, very good writers."

Several dissertation advisors, in fact, commented that it is more difficult to write a good nontraditional dissertation, and that it demands better than usual writing skills from the candidate. While this approach may not seem exactly fair, as these same dissertation advisors supervise traditional qualitative dissertations that are not very well written, students need to know that this is something to face. It is a reality that when you do research, you are part of a socially organized process. Traditions provide pathways that dissertation advisors are accustomed to traversing, and even if a more traditional qualitative dissertation is not elegantly written, it is constructed in a way that provides easy access for the committee. If you want to travel down one of the new pathways or strengthen the alternative forms of work, you need to think of your work not just as scholarship about a particular subject area, but also as addressing the form of the work. You need to be especially well prepared to answer questions about methodological rigor, defined as the reader's knowing why you, the researcher, know what you know or claim what you claim. While there is no guarantee that such an explanation makes for a better dissertation, it is one of the demands of the relationship between reader and author. And you may have to respond to queries about why the reader should care about the personal stories in your dissertation.

Professional considerations are also a significant issue. The dissertation is a document that can follow you on your career path. Questions about your professional identity are something to consider, as is the issue of credibility. There are additional burdens of credibility that come for you as a doctoral student when you use nontraditional forms. Extra work is required to successfully complete a nontraditional dissertation. This kind of work involves a higher level of self-consciousness in explaining the choices you have made to your readers. Readers familiar with the qualitative approach know what you are doing when you write within tradition but will need extra guidance when you are doing more experimental work. Some faculty believe that in order to do nontraditional work well, you must know what the traditions are. One advisor described the qualitative approach as "an apprenticeship within a tradition." All of the advisors we spoke to for this chapter said that nontraditional methods need to advance the story more than would be necessary in a dissertation written using more traditional qualitative approaches.

The experimental writer also must consider how to connect writings about self to larger issues, to the "big ideas" that the project addresses. Clair (2003) insists that the "approach demands that the personal narrative move beyond the individual and develop connections with the culture" (xii). Put another way, when you include personal material in your dissertation, you need to ask yourself, Why is it here? How does it serve my project? Lincoln and Denzin (2003) in their discussion of doing qualitative research during the "crisis of legitimation" frame the issue according to the relationship between the researcher and the informants. They say that we must ask several questions about the "authority of the text." These include: "Is a text . . . faithful to the context and the individuals it is supposed to represent? Does the text have the right to assert that it is a report to the larger world that addresses not only the researchers' interests, but also the interests of those studied?" (pp. 618–619). There are a variety of ways to respond to these questions, and nontraditional approaches have also developed responses (see, e.g., Richardson, 2003; Ellis, 1997, 2004).

If you are attracted to doing a nontraditional qualitative dissertation, you might think of the vocabulary that is available to discuss such an undertaking. The textual turn in ethnography, a shift affected by postmodernism, influenced researchers to emphasize textual practices as much as fieldwork. From this movement came the language of "tales" to describe different narrative forms of representation (Van Maanen, 1988) and the language of reflexivity and social location (Hertz, 1997). Critical race theory promotes the telling of personal stories and narratives as central to a qualitative approach that emphasizes the space that the lives of people of color need to occupy (Duncan, 2002; Ladson-Billings, 2003). Feminist and antiracist work that addresses the relationship between researchers and the Others they represent has been described as "working the hyphens" (Fine, 1994). Richardson (2000) has argued for more innovative writing, not only to address issues differently but also to challenge what we can write about. She suggests a form of what DeVault (1997) calls "rhetorical innovation" to challenge social science itself. Richardson (2000) describes "evocative writing" as a method to investigate "how standard objectifying practices of social science necessarily limit us and social science" (p. 5). There are, in other words, many people doing scholarship who use nontraditional methods, who teach about it, and who provide students space in classes to write papers using this approach.

ADVICE

What is our advice for you about whether to attempt a nontraditional dissertation? We are not wholeheartedly advocating for this approach; we take a much more cautious stance. We see the dangers of the approach for this particular research exercise. It is a complicated decision. At the same time, we have heard many stories of superb dissertations using fictional components that worked well, and we have read dissertations using critical race theory that wove rich personal narratives throughout the text. You might do some homework first, as we did to prepare for writing this chapter. Look in *Dissertation Abstracts* for scholars whose work represents nontraditional qualitative scholarship, and then examine their students' dissertations. What universities and degree programs support such scholarship? You can get ideas and support from them. Passion for your scholarship is an important piece of the dissertation process. If you are passionate about writing a nontraditional dissertation, do the homework that will help you find support for doing such work well.

Finally, nontraditional dissertations may all be nontraditional, but they approach their form in quite different ways. As a reader, I am much more interested in hearing a personal story if I know why I am hearing it, and what purpose it serves. I am less interested if I am unclear about why I should care about the narrator's life. Do I need to know that the narrator spoke on the phone to someone when she was working out how to write the article or represent some informants? If we underestimate the writing skills that are involved in "evocative writing," we may not communicate in an innovative way that challenges drier social science writing, but rather bore our readers.

References

Abu-Lughod, L. (2005). *Dramas of nationhood: The politics of television in Egypt.* Chicago: University of Chicago Press.

Alcoff, L. (1991/1992). The problem of speaking for others. *Cultural Critique, 23,* 5–32.

Atkinson, P., Coffey, A., & Delamont, S. (2003). *Key themes in qualitative research.* Walnut Creek, CA: AltaMira Press.

Banks, C. (2004). *This is how we do it: Black undergraduate women's perspectives on cultural contexts in higher education.* Unpublished dissertation proposal, Syracuse University.

Banks, C. (2006). *This is how we do it! Black women undergraduates, cultural capital and college success—reworking discourse.* Unpublished doctoral dissertation, Syracuse University, Syracuse, NY.

Bannister, J. (2001). *"Home-work": Difference and (em)power(ment) in parent involvement discourse.* Unpublished doctoral dissertation, Syracuse University, Syracuse, NY.

Becker, H. (1970). *Sociological work.* Chicago: Aldine

Becker, H. (1986). *Writing for social scientists.* Chicago: University of Chicago Press.

Best, A. (1998). *Schooling and the production of popular culture: Negotiating subjectivities at the high school prom.* Unpublished doctoral dissertation, Syracuse University, Syracuse, NY.

Best, A. (2000). *Prom night.* New York: Routledge.

Biklen, S. (1995). *School work: Gender and the cultural construction of teaching.* New York: Teachers College Press.

Biklen, S. (2004). Trouble on memory lane: Adults and self-retrospection in researching youth. *Qualitative Inquiry, 10*(5), 715–730.

Bogad, L. (2002). *Feed your mind: A qualitative study of youth, power and privilege.* Unpublished doctoral dissertation, Syracuse University, Syracuse, NY.

Bogdan, R. (1976). National policy and situated meaning: The case of Headstart and the handicapped. *American Journal of Orthopsychiatry, 46*(2), 229–235.

Bogdan, R., & Biklen, S. (2007). *Qualitative research for education* (5th ed.). Boston: Allyn & Bacon.

Bogdan, R., Brown, M. A., & Foster, S. (1982). Be honest but not cruel: Staff/parent communication on neonatal units. *Human Organization, 41*(1), 6–16.

Bogdan, R., & Taylor, S. (1994). *The social meaning of mental retardation.* New York: Teachers College Press.

Bourdieu, P. (1977). *Outline of a theory of practice.* Cambridge, UK: Cambridge University Press.

Bourdieu, P. (1984). *Distinction—A social critique of the judgment of taste.* (R. Nice, Trans.). Cambridge, MA: Harvard University Press.

Bourdieu, P. (1997). The forms of capital. In A. H. Halsey, H. Lauder, P. Brown, & A. S. Wells (Eds.), *Education: Culture, economy, society* (pp. 46–58). Oxford: Oxford University Press.

Bourdieu, P., & Wacquant, L. (1992). *An invitation to reflexive sociology.* Chicago: University of Chicago Press.

Campbell, M., & Gregor, F. (2004). *Mapping social relations: A primer in doing institutional ethnography.* Walnut Creek, CA: AltaMira Press.

Casella, R. (1997). *Popular education and pedagogy in everyday life: The nature of educational travel in the Americas.* Unpublished doctoral dissertation, Syracuse University, Syracuse, NY.

Casella, R. (2006). *Selling us the fortress.* New York: Routledge.

Clair, R. P. (Ed.). (2003). *Expressions of ethnography: Novel approaches to qualitative methods.* Albany: State University of New York Press.

Davis, J. (1992). Tense in ethnography: Some practical considerations. In J. Okely & H. Callaway (Eds.), *Anthropology & autobiography* (pp. 205–220). London: Routledge.

De Andrade, L. (2000). Negotiating from the inside: Constructing racial and ethnic identity in qualitative research. *Journal of Contemporary Ethnography, 29*(3), 268–290.

Denzin, N., & Lincoln, Y. (Eds.). (1994). *Handbook of qualitative research.* Thousand Oaks, CA: Sage.

DeVault, M. (1997). Personal writing in social research. In R. Hertz (Ed.), *Reflexivity and voice* (pp. 216–228). Thousand Oaks, CA: Sage.

DeVault, M. (1999). *Liberating method: Feminism and social research.* Philadelphia: Temple University Press.

DeVault, M., & McCoy, L. (2002). Institutional ethnography: Using interviews to investigate ruling relations. In J. Gubrium & J. Holstein (Eds.), *Handbook of interview research* (pp. 751–756). Thousand Oaks, CA: Sage.

Duncan, G. A. (2002). Critical race theory and method: Rendering race in urban ethnographic research. *Qualitative Inquiry, 8*(1), 85–104.

Edgar, A., & Sedgwick, P. (1999). *Key concepts in cultural theory.* London: Routledge.

Ellis, C. (1991). Sociological introspection and emotional experience. *Symbolic Interaction, 14,* 23–50.

Ellis, C. (1997). Evocative autoethnography: Writing emotionally about our lives. In W. Tierney & Y. Lincoln (Eds.), *Representation and the text: Re-framing the narrative voice* (pp. 115–142). Albany: State University of New York Press.

Ellis, C. (2004). *The ethnographic I: A methodological novel about autoethnography.* Walnut Creek, CA: AltaMira Press.

Esposito, J. (2002). *Lotions and potions: The meanings college women make of everyday experiences of femininities.* Unpublished doctoral dissertation, Syracuse University, Syracuse, NY.

Ferri, B. (1997). *Construction of identity among women with learning disabilities: The many faces of the self.* Unpublished doctoral dissertation, University of Georgia, Athens, GA.

Fine, M. (1994). Working the hyphens: Reinventing self and other in qualitative research. In N. Denzin & Y. Lincoln (Eds.), *Handbook of Qualitative Research* (pp. 70–82). Thousand Oaks, CA: Sage.

Flower-Kim, K. (2005). *We are family: Trans-racial adoption and the work of assembling and practicing family (Korea).* Unpublished doctoral dissertation, Syracuse University, Syracuse, NY.

Foley, D. (1990). *Learning capitalist culture.* Philadelphia: University of Pennsylvania Press.

Geer, B. (1964). First days in the field. In P. Hammond (Ed.), *Sociologists at work* (pp. 372–398). New York: Basic Books.

Geertz, C. (1995). *After the fact.* Cambridge, MA: Harvard University Press.

Goodall, H. L., Jr. (2000). *Writing the new ethnography.* Walnut Creek, CA: AltaMira Press.

Gregory, K. (2003). *The everyday lives of sex workers in the Netherlands.* Unpublished doctoral dissertation, Syracuse University, Syracuse, NY.

Gupta, A., & Ferguson, J. (1997). Discipline and practice: "The field" as a site, method, and location in anthropology. In A. Gupta & J. Ferguson (Eds.), *Anthropological locations* (pp. 1–46). Berkeley: University of California Press.

Haraway, D. (1988). Situated knowledge: The science question in feminism and the privilege of partial perspective. *Feminist Studies, 14,* 575–599.

Haraway, D. (1991). *Simians, cyborgs and women: The reinvention of nature.* New York: Routledge.

Hemmings, A. (2006). Great ethical divides: Bridging the gap between institutional review boards and researchers. *Educational Researcher, 35*(1), 12–18.

Herrera, C. D. (1999). Two arguments for "covert methods" in social research. *British Journal of Sociology, 50*(2), 331–343.

Hertz, R. (Ed.). (1997). *Reflexivity and voice.* Thousand Oaks, CA: Sage.

Hochschild, A. (1983). *The managed heart.* Berkeley: University of California Press.

Johns, M., Chen, S. S., & Hall, J. (Eds.). (2004). *Online social research.* New York: Peter Lang.

Jones, J. (1993). *Bad blood: The Tuskegee syphilis experiment.* New York: Free Press.

King, S. (2002). *On writing.* New York: Pocket Books.

Kliewer, C. (1995). *The social representation of children with Down syndrome: An interpretive analysis.* Unpublished doctoral dissertation, Syracuse University, Syracuse, NY.

Ladson-Billings, G. (2003). It's your world, I'm just trying to explain it: Understanding our epistemological and methodological challenges. *Qualitative Inquiry, 9*(1), 5–12.

Lareau, A. (1989). *Home advantage.* London: Falmer.

Lareau, A., & Shultz, J. (Eds.). (1996). *Journeys through ethnography*. Boulder, CO: Westview.

Lather, P., & Smithies, C. (1997). *Troubling the angels*. Boulder, CO: Westview Press.

Lesko, N. (2001). *Act your age!* New York: Routledge Falmer.

Lincoln, Y., & Denzin, N. (2003). The seventh moment: Out of the past. In N. Denzin & Y. Lincoln (Eds.), *The landscape of qualitative research* (2nd ed., pp. 611–640). Thousand Oaks, CA: Sage.

Luschen, K. (2005). *Empowering prevention? Adolescent female sexuality, advocacy, and schooling*. Unpublished doctoral dissertation, Syracuse University, Syracuse, NY.

Mangram, J. (2006). *Struggles over meaning: Social studies teachers' perspectives of media and popular culture*. Unpublished doctoral dissertation, Syracuse University, Syracuse, NY.

Marcus, G. (1998). *Ethnography through thick and thin*. Princeton, NJ: Princeton University Press.

McGowan, K. (2001). *Rinsing off the soap: Cultural hierarchy and the search for legitimacy in daytime drama production*. Unpublished doctoral dissertation, Syracuse University, Syracuse, NY.

Mills, C. W. (1959). *The sociological imagination*. New York: Oxford University Press.

Mischler, E. (1979). Meaning in context: Is there any other kind? *Harvard Educational Review, 49*(1), 1–19.

Mitford, J. (1979). *Poison penmanship*. New York: Random House.

Nathan, R. (2005a, July 29). An anthropologist goes undercover. *The Chronicle of Higher Education, 51*.

Nathan, R. (2005b). *My freshman year: What a professor learned by becoming a student*. Ithaca, NY: Cornell University Press.

Nelson, L. W. (1996). "Hands in the chit'lins": Notes on native anthropological research among African American women. In G. Etter-Lewis & M. Foster (Eds.), *Unrelated kin: Race and gender in women's personal narratives* (pp. 183–199). New York: Routledge.

Reverby, S. (Ed.). (2000). *Tuskegee's truths*. Chapel Hill: University of North Carolina Press.

Richardson, L. (2000). New writing practices in qualitative research. *Sociology of Sport, 17*: 5–20.

Richardson, L. (2003). Writing, a method of inquiry. In N. Denzin & Y. Lincoln (Eds.), *Collecting and interpreting qualitative materials* (2nd ed., pp. 499–541). Thousand Oaks, CA: Sage.

Riley, R. (2000). *Hidden soldiers: Gender, militarism and the discourse of defense*. Unpublished doctoral dissertation, Syracuse University, Syracuse, NY.

Rist, R. C. (1980). "Blitzkrieg ethnography": On the transformation of a method into a movement. *Educational Researcher, 9*(2), 8–10.

Rubin, H., & Rubin, I. (1995). *Qualitative interviewing*. Thousand Oaks, CA: Sage.

Schwartz, M. (2006). *Communication in the doctor's office: Deaf patients talk about their physicians*. Unpublished doctoral dissertation, Syracuse University, Syracuse, NY.

Smith, D. (1987). *The everyday world as problematic.* Boston: Northeastern University Press.

Smith, D. (1990). K is mentally ill. In Smith, *Texts, facts and femininity* (pp. 12–51). London: Routledge.

Smith, D. (2005). *Institutional ethnography: A sociology for people.* Lanham, MD: AltaMira Press.

Smith, L. (1999). *Decolonizing methodologies.* London: Zed Books.

Solomon, B. (1999). *An illusion of difference: Reconstituting women on welfare into the working poor.* Unpublished doctoral dissertation, Syracuse University, Syracuse, NY.

Solorzano, D., & Yosso, T. (2002). Critical race methodology: Counter-storytelling as an analytical framework for education research. *Qualitative Inquiry, 8*(1), 23–44.

Steet, L. (1993). *Teaching orientalism in American popular education:* National Geographic, *1888–1988.* Unpublished doctoral dissertation, Syracuse University, Syracuse, NY.

Strunk, W., & White, E. B. (2000). *The elements of style* (4th ed.). New York: Longman.

Swaminathan, R. (1997). *"The charming sideshow": Cheerleading, girls' culture and schooling.* Unpublished doctoral dissertation, Syracuse University, Syracuse, NY.

Taylor, S. (2006). Personal communication.

Thomas, W. I. (1923). *The unadjusted girl.* Boston: Little, Brown.

Thorne, B. (1993). *Gender play.* New Brunswick, NJ: Rutgers University Press.

Van Maanen, J. (1988). *Tales of the field.* Chicago: University of Chicago Press.

Villenas, S. (1996). The colonizer/colonized Chicana ethnographer: Identity, marginalization, and co-optation in the field. *Harvard Educational Review, 66*(4), 711–731.

Waldron, L. (2002). *In the wake of Columbine: How youth make meaning of violence, schooling and the media.* Unpublished doctoral dissertation, Syracuse University, Syracuse, NY.

Watson, C. W. (Ed.). (1999). *Being there.* London: Pluto Press.

Wexler, D. (2003). *Shifting pedagogies: Intersections of computer supported technologies, education and power.* Unpublished doctoral dissertation, Syracuse University, Syracuse, NY.

Wolf, D. (Ed.). (1996). *Feminist dilemmas in fieldwork.* Boulder, CO: Westview.

Zuckerman, J. B. (2001). *Queering the life of a progressive, urban elementary school: Genealogical ghost stories.* Unpublished doctoral dissertation, Teachers College, Columbia University, New York.

Resource Guide

BASICS OF QUALITATIVE METHODS

Bogdan, R., & Biklen, S. (2007). *Qualitative research for education* (5th ed.). Boston: Allyn & Bacon.

Denzin, N., & Lincoln, Y. (2003). *Collecting and interpreting qualitative materials* (2nd ed.). Thousand Oaks, CA: Sage.

Emerson, R., Fretz, R., & Shaw, L. (1995). *Writing ethnographic fieldnotes.* Chicago: University of Chicago Press.

Taylor, S., & Bogdan, R. (1998). *Introduction to qualitative research methods* (3rd ed.). New York: Wiley.

INTERVIEWING

Briggs, C. (1986). *Learning how to ask.* Cambridge, England: Cambridge University Press.

Hollway, W., & Jefferson, T. (2000). *Doing qualitative research differently: Free association, narrative, and the interview method.* London: Sage.

Mishler, E. (1986). *Research interviewing: Context and narrative.* Cambridge, MA: Harvard University Press.

Rubin, H., & Rubin, I. (2005). *Qualitative interviewing. The art of hearing data.* Thousand Oaks, CA: Sage.

WRITING

Becker, H. (1986). *Writing for social scientists.* Chicago: University of Chicago Press.

Krieger, S. (1991). *Social science and the self.* New Brunswick, NJ: Rutgers University Press.

Van Maanen, J. (1988). *Tales of the field: On writing ethnography.* Chicago: University of Chicago Press.

Richardson, L. (1994). Writing: A method of inquiry. In N. Denzin & Y. Lincoln (Eds.), *Handbook of Qualitative Research* (pp. 516–529). Thousand Oaks, CA: Sage.

EXAMPLES OF BOOKS BASED
ON QUALITATIVE DISSERTATIONS

*(First names are given so that you can look up
the dissertations in* Dissertation Abstracts.)

Best, Amy. (2000). *Prom night*. New York: Routledge.

Bettie, Julie. (2003). *Women without class*. Berkeley: University of California Press.

Gregory, Katherine. (2005). *The everyday lives of sex workers in the Netherlands*. New York: Routledge.

Linneman, R. Daniel. (2001). *Idiots: Stories about mindedness and mental retardation*. New York: Peter Lang.

Kliewer, Chris. (1998). *Schooling children with Down syndrome*. New York: Teachers College Press.

Linden, R. Ruth. (1993). *Making stories, making selves*. Columbus: Ohio State University Press.

Oyler, Celia. (1996). *Making room for students*. New York: Teachers College Press.

Perry, Pamela. (2002). *Shades of white: White kids and racial identity in high school*. Durham, NC: Duke University Press.

Steet, Linda. (2000). *Veils and daggers*. Philadelphia: Temple University Press.

EXAMPLES OF JOURNALS DEVOTED
TO QUALITATIVE METHODS

International Journal of Qualitative Studies in Education (QSE)
Qualitative Sociology
Journal of Contemporary Ethnography
Qualitative Inquiry
Studies in Symbolic Interaction
Field Methods
Ethnography and Education

WEBSITES ON QUALITATIVE METHODS

http://www.qualitative-research.net/fqs/fqs-eng.htm. (Forum Qualitative Social Research [FQS])

http://www.qsrinternational.com/

http://www.audiencedialogue.org/soft-qual.html

http://www.intute.ac.uk/socialsciences/cgi-bin/browse.pl?id=120997 (papers on all aspects of qualitative methods)
http://wings.buffalo.edu/soc-sci/sociology/.SGSA/qrls.html (source for qualitative listserves)
http://www.uga.edu/squig/listservs.html (source for qualitative listserves)

VOICE, RACE, SUBJECTIVITY, POLITICS, AND QUALITATIVE METHODS

Collins, P. H. (1990). *Black feminist thought*. New York: Routledge.
Denzin, N., & Lincoln, Y. (Eds.). (2003). *The landscape of qualitative research*. Thousand Oaks, CA: Sage.
DeVault, M. (1999). *Liberating method: Feminism and social research*. Philadelphia: Temple University Press.
Hertz, R. (Ed.). (1997). *Reflexivity and voice*. Thousand Oaks, CA: Sage.
Marcus, G., & Fischer, M. (1986). *Anthopology as cultural critique*. Chicago: University of Chicago Press.
Twine, F., & Warren, J. (Eds.). (2000). *Racing research, researching race*. New York: New York University Press.
Wolf, D. (Ed.). (1996). *Feminist dilemmas in fieldwork*. Boulder, CO: Westview Press.

MULTIPLE QUALITATIVE METHODS

Campbell, M., & Gregor, F. (2004). *Mapping social relations: A primer in doing institutional ethnography*. Walnut Creek, CA: AltaMira Press.
DeVault, M., & McCoy, L. (2002). Institutional ethnography: Using interviews to investigate ruling relations. In J. Gubrium & J. Holstein (Eds.), *Handbook of interview research* (pp. 751–756). Thousand Oaks, CA: Sage.
Johns, M., Chen, S., & Hall, G. (Eds.). (2004). *Online social research*. New York: Peter Lang.
Linde, C. (1993). *Life stories*. New York: Oxford University Press.
Prosser, J. (Ed.). (1998). *Image-based research: A sourcebook for qualitative researchers*. London: Falmer Press.

POINT OF VIEW: CONSTRUCTING THE SUBJECTIVITY-OBJECTIVITY RELATIONSHIP

Berger, P., & Luckmann, T. (1967). *The social construction of reality*. Garden City, NJ: Doubleday.
Clifford, J., & Marcus, G. (Eds.). (1986). *The predicament of culture*. Berkeley: University of California Press.
Haraway, D. (1991). Situated knowledges: The science question in feminism and

the privilege of partial perspective. In Haraway, *Simians, cyborgs, and women* (pp. 183–201). NY: Routledge.

NONTRADITIONAL QUALITATIVE METHODS

Clair, R. P. (Ed.). (2003). *Expressions of ethnography: Novel approaches to qualitative methods*. Albany: State University of New York Press.
Denzin, N. (2003). *Performance ethnography*. Thousand Oaks, CA: Sage.
Ellis, C., & Bochner, A. (Eds.). (1996). *Composing ethnography: Alternative forms of qualitative writing*. Walnut Creek, CA: AltaMira Press.
Lincoln, Y., & Denzin, N. (2003). *Turning points in qualitative research*. Walnut Creek, CA: AltaMira Press.

Index

About the Authors

Sari Knopp Biklen is Laura and Douglas Meredith Professor and Chair of Cultural Foundations of Education, Syracuse University. She has written *Qualitative Research for Education* with Robert Bogdan (5th ed., 2007), and *School Work: Gender and the Cultural Construction of Teaching* (1995) and has edited several collections. She was an American Association of University Women University Scholar, and she directs the Institute on Popular Culture and Education. Her articles have been published in such journals as *Qualitative Inquiry, Teacher's College Record, Qualitative Studies in Education, History of Education Review, Teacher Education Quarterly,* and *Educational Studies.* Her interests include qualitative research methods, gender and representation, multiculturalism, popular culture, and adolescence. She won the Willystine Goodsell award from the American Educational Research Association for her scholarship on women.

Ronnie Casella is Associate Professor of Education at Central Connecticut State University and Research Fellow at the University of the Witwatersrand in Johannesburg, South Africa. His most recent book is *Selling Us the Fortress: The Promotion of Techno-Security Equipment for Schools.* He has published articles in the *International Journal of Qualitative Studies in Education, Anthropology and Education Quarterly, Social Justice, Teachers College Record, The Urban Review,* and other journals. In 2006 he was Visiting Scholar at the University of the Witwatersrand, where his research focused on school and youth violence in Johannesburg and Soweto. He teaches classes on comparative and international education, the sociology of education, and qualitative research. His writings focus on youth and school violence, education in a global context, and relationships between schools and private businesses, NGOs, and community organizations. He received his M.A. in English Education from New York University and his Ph.D. in Cultural Foundations of Education at Syracuse University, where his dissertation focused on educational travel organizations that feature trips to Latin America. Sari Biklen was Chair of the dissertation committee.